A MUSLI[M]
FAMILY[ ]
IN BRITA[IN]

GW00746091

A MUSLIM FAMILY IN BRITAIN

Stephen W. Harrison and David Shepherd

Illustrated by
James Val

Religious Education Press
A Division of Pergamon Press

ACKNOWLEDGEMENTS

It would be impossible in a book of this nature to acknowledge all who have helped in its production. We would, however, like to mention the following:

The Pakistan Embassy

The Chief Education Officer, Headteachers and Staff of Lancashire Local Education Authority

Mr J. L. Fallows (Lancashire County Adviser) and Miss R. J. Wells (Curriculum Development Officer, Lancashire County)

Mr G. M. Bowder (Department of Arabic and Islamic Studies, University of Lancaster)

The committee of the Hanfi Sunni Muslim Circle, Preston, and, in particular, the former imam, Mr S. Khan

The committee of the Preston Muslim Society, especially Mr Y. S. Limbada, former vice-president and secretary of the Society

Mr Peter Woodward, General Inspector of Schools, with responsibility for religious education in the City of Birmingham, for reading, and commenting so constructively on, the first draft of the book.

Muslim pupils, past and present, without whom many ideas for this book would not have germinated.

But in the final analysis it is the authors who must be held responsible for any textual errors.

Qur'anic quotations in the text are taken from M. M. Pickthall, *The Meaning of the Glorious Koran*. Mentor Religious Classic. New English Library (paperback).

Stephen W. Harrison is Headteacher at Revoe Junior School, Blackpool, Lancashire

David Shepherd is Headteacher at Hanslope County Combined School, Milton Keynes, Buckinghamshire

To Pat

THE RELIGIOUS EDUCATION PRESS
A Division of Pergamon Press
Hennock Road, Exeter EX2 8RP
Copyright © 1980   Stephen W. Harrison and David Shepherd
All Rights Reserved

First published 1980, reprinted 1980, 1982

Printed in Great Britain by A. Wheaton & Co. Ltd, Exeter (T.S.)
ISBN 0 08 022884 4 non net   ISBN 0 08 022885 2 net

In This Book

Foreword

Reading *A Muslim Family in Britain* took me back to my childhood many years ago in South Africa. I grew up there in a multicultural society amongst Hindus, Jews, Malays, Africans and Muslims. My father, himself a devout Muslim and an imam, encouraged us to understand and respect our own religion, whilst at the same time, learning about the beliefs and customs of those around us who were not Muslims. How right he was! To this day I often remember his teachings.

We all live now in what has been termed a global village, a world in which no longer can there be far-off peoples of whom we know little. It is vital as never before that we and our children learn about human diversity of culture and religion in order that brotherhood and peace based on mutual respect can flourish. If we should fail in this task we know only too well what the consequences can be.

I hope that teachers who use this book (and also its companion volumes in the series) will remember that ethnic communities in Britain are only too pleased to provide visiting speakers and take guests on visits to mosques and similar places. Contact can be made directly, or if in doubt, through the local Community Relations Council. Education is a lifelong experience that flourishes through bonds of friendship between communities.

I am sure those who use this book will delight in journeying through the world of Islam. Such delights were mine when I was a child in South Africa first learning of the cultural riches around me. This, too, can be the experience of the young in Britain today.

Sm. Ahamed

SAYED M. AHAMED
Principal Community Relations Officer
Manchester Council for Community Relations

1 A Visit to the Airport

Idris and Peter had always looked forward to the occasions when their teacher was to take their class on a visit to some place of interest. Today's outing was no exception. They were going to Manchester International Airport.

The journey from school in Preston to the airport did not seem to take long. Once in Manchester, Idris and Peter listened to their teacher as he explained the different workings of a busy airport. Afterwards the two boys were free to chat to one another.

Peter: "Did you once tell me that you had been to this airport before?"

Idris: "Yes, I have."

Peter: "When was that?"

Idris: "I first came ten years ago with my mother, when we emigrated from our home in Pakistan."

Peter: "Ten years ago? You must have been very young."

Idris: "Yes, that's right. I was only four years old then. My sister, Fatima, was born about a year after we emigrated. She is now aged nine."

Peter: "You mentioned that you emigrated to Britain with your mother, but what about your father? Didn't he come with you as well?"

Idris: "No, he was already here—he'd emigrated about two years before."

Idris and Peter were unable to continue talking because their teacher began to point out the places to which aeroplanes fly from Manchester. They were able to pick up the threads of their conversation later on the coach journey back to school.

9

The Hussein family

Peter: "When we were at the airport, Idris, you told me that you first came to Manchester with your mother. Does that mean you've been there since?"

Idris: "Oh yes, lots of times. My father always likes to take me to the airport with him if he is meeting any of our relatives or friends who are travelling between Britain and Pakistan. I remember when my mother and I first arrived here we were welcomed by a number of our relatives and friends who were already living in Britain—not just by my father."

Peter: "Have you ever been back to Pakistan?"

Idris: "Yes, twice—once when I was nine, and last year when I was thirteen. My father took me."

Peter: "Has Fatima ever been there?"

Idris: "No. Although he has no firm plans yet, my father hopes she'll be able to go there some day—perhaps with my mother."

Although Idris and Peter had been good friends since they left their different primary schools just over three years ago, Peter had never asked Idris very much about his family. Now, however, many questions were springing to his mind. He wanted to know why families like the Husseins came to Britain and what Pakistan was like. He had also noticed that Idris and Fatima often spoke about the **mosque**. But he did not know what one looked like inside nor what the people who went there believed. In the same way he was interested in how Muslims lived at home. He had heard such peculiar stories from his English friends that he wanted to find out more for himself.

Peter's curiosity had been aroused, but as the coach was now approaching Preston he would have to wait to have these questions answered.

11

2 Why Britain?

Fortunately for Peter he did not have to wait long before some of his questions were answered. This was mainly because his teacher decided to follow up the visit to the airport with a lesson on why immigrants decide to come to Britain.

Peter was very interested in this subject and noted down the main points his teacher made. The first of these was that there has been a general increase in travel during the past ten years or so. People travel by car, ship or aeroplane more now than ever before. Added to this, Peter's teacher pointed out that man has always liked travelling. The Bible stories of Abraham and Moses illustrate this, as does the fact that Britain itself comprises a mixture of peoples. Angles, Saxons, Jutes, Vikings, Danes, Normans and the like, as well as more recent immigrants, came to this country for many different reasons, but they have all shared a liking for travel.

Peter also jotted down an historical reason for many immigrants settling in Britain. At one time many countries in the world, including Pakistan, helped to make up the British Empire. The peoples living in these countries often regarded Britain affectionately and thought of it as their motherland, even though they had never been there. Some of them would have learned to speak English at school as well as studying much about the British way of life from their books at school. It seems quite natural, therefore, that when such people wanted to emigrate, many of them chose Britain. On the other hand, Peter's teacher did point out

12

that not all emigrants choose to come to Britain. For instance, many Pakistanis have gone to various other parts of the world.

Yet in spite of these factors, it seems that the major reasons for immigrants coming to Britain are to do with education and money. Many immigrants, and this is true of a large number of Pakistanis, have little chance of getting a good education in their own countries. There are simply not enough secondary schools in many places to cater for all the children who wish to go to them. Consequently a large number are unable to have any secondary education at all. Many parents wish to emigrate so that their children can receive such an education. They realise that without proper education their children will be unable to get good jobs and will therefore be poorly paid when they start working.

Towards the end of the lesson Peter's teacher suggested that those English children who were interested should ask some of their immigrant friends why their families settled in Britain. Peter thought this was a good idea but did not get a chance to talk to his friend Idris until they were on their way home from school.

Peter: "Why did your family emigrate, Idris?"

Idris: "Well, my father was really fed up with being poor in Pakistan. He said the only way we could improve our standard of living was to come to Britain."

Peter: "But why Britain?"

Idris: "Well, at that time a number of my father's relatives and friends had emigrated to this country. They wrote and said that they had all managed to find jobs, buy houses, and that the schools were good. They also told my father that they were now earning more in one week than they could earn in Pakistan in a whole year. This was even the case with one or two of my father's friends who were graduates from Pakistani universities. These friends now work alongside my father in a textile factory. My father says that sometimes they don't like doing so because they think they are capable of doing better jobs. Unfortunately

13

for them, however, their Pakistani degrees are not recognised in Britain in the same way as British degrees, so they are unlikely to get the sorts of jobs they would like."

Peter: "Did your father's relatives and friends all settle in Preston?"

Idris: "Yes, I guess that was why we came here."

Peter: "You told me at the airport that your father came to Britain about two years ahead of the rest of your family. Why was that?"

Idris: "Many families emigrated from Pakistan in this way at that time, and some still do. They do so for two reasons. In the first place, they often can't afford to bring their families over by air all at once. Also, if the fathers come here first and get jobs, they can save up enough money to buy a house, so that when their families do arrive in Britain they have a home to come to. When my father first arrived here he lived in a house with a number of other Pakistani fathers who, like him, were saving up to buy houses. Together like this, they could all live cheaply and save up fairly quickly."

Peter: "You said that some Pakistani families still emigrate in this way. What about those who don't?"

Idris: "Some emigrate as complete families nowadays. This is often because they have relatives or friends in Britain who lend them the money they need for the fare, as well as letting them rent a house from them until they can buy one of their own. In fact, nearly all of my Indian friends at the mosque emigrated as complete families."

Peter: "Do you think you'll ever go back and live in Pakistan when you are older?"

Idris: "No, and I don't think Fatima will either. You see, we've been brought up in Britain and we see ourselves as British. We enjoy living here with our friends and really don't want to make our homes in Pakistan."

Peter: "Will your parents ever go back and live there?"

Idris: "No, I don't think so. Mind you, some of my father's relatives and friends would like to. Some of them

14

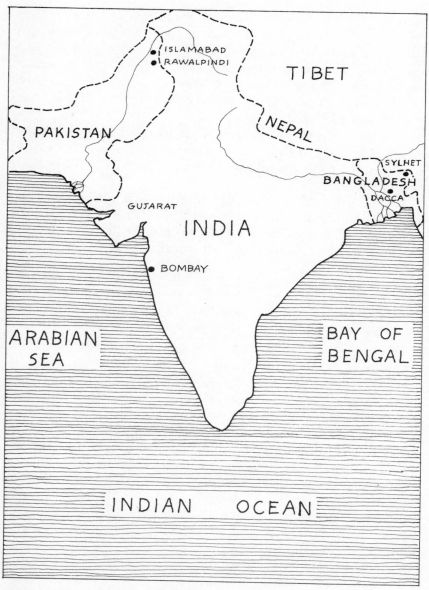

Main areas of origin of Muslims living in Britain—Pakistan, Bangladesh and the State of Gujarat

have sent a lot of money back to members of their families who are still there to enable them to buy a nice house and plenty of land. But in spite of this, they don't find it easy to return. This is because their children, like Fatima and myself, see themselves as British and have no wish to give up their way of life, which is the only one they know, to go and live in Pakistan."

At that point the boys arrived at Idris's house. Idris had enjoyed talking to Peter so much that he thought he would invite him in for a while so that they could continue their conversation.

Idris: "Would you like to come in for a while, and then I'll tell you about where we used to live in Pakistan?"

Peter: "Thanks, that would be nice, but I mustn't be too long or else my mother will wonder where I am."

3 The Husseins' Life in Pakistan

Peter had not been in Idris's house long before Mrs Hussein asked the boys if they would like a drink and a biscuit. Since they were rather hungry after their day at school, they thanked Mrs Hussein and said that they would.

Idris told his father, who had joined the boys for a cup of tea, that he was going to talk to Peter about their home in Pakistan. As Idris himself had spent most of his life in Britain, he asked his father if he would like to join in the conversation. Mr Hussein always liked talking about Pakistan, so was glad of this opportunity to do so.

Idris: "Peter asks a lot of questions you know, Dad."

Mr Hussein: "Well, I don't mind. After all, I am always answering yours, Idris."

Peter: "Well, I might as well begin. Whereabouts did you live in Pakistan?"

Idris: "In a little village just outside Rawalpindi in the Punjab."

Peter: "What was the village like?"

Mr Hussein: "I think I had better answer this question. It was small, with only a few hundred people living there. The roads weren't like those in Britain—they could only be called tracks by British standards because they were so rough. That did not really matter though, because only a few cars and tractors used them."

Peter: "Do all Pakistanis live in small villages?"

17

Mr Hussein: "Oh no. In fact, Rawalpindi is a big industrial town with a population of some 1¾ million people."

Peter: "Goodness, that's nearly twice as big as Birmingham. What are the roads like in Rawalpindi?"

Mr Hussein: "They are as well made as many British roads. You see, many people work in the shops, offices and factories of Rawalpindi—the Army even has its headquarters there—thus creating the need for much transport. Consequently many buses and cars use the roads."

Peter: "Did you go into Rawalpindi often?"

Mr Hussein: "No, not really. You see, I used to work on a small farm which belonged to me. The soil was not very good and we were generally poor. We just couldn't afford our own transport. We tended to go to Rawalpindi only when relatives or friends could take us. But we all flew to Britain from Rawalpindi Airport."

Peter: "What was your house like, Mr Hussein?"

Mr Hussein: "It was made of mud and stone and thatched with grass. It was very small and we often had one or two of our farm animals in the house as well. We had some furniture, but not very much."

Peter: "Did you have electricity and water?"

Mr Hussein: "Unfortunately no—but many people do in Pakistan. In fact, in Rawalpindi nearly everyone does."

Peter: "How did you manage, then?"

Mr Hussein: "We used lamps and a well."

Peter: "What is the weather like there? I imagine it's always hot."

Idris: "Well, that is not strictly true. In the winter the weather can be cold. In fact, the temperature at that time of the year ranges from 6 °C to 37 °C. In summer, however, it can become very hot—from 12 °C up to as high as 47 °C."

Peter: "Does it rain much?"

Mr Hussein: "Yes, especially during the months from June to September. We call this the monsoon period, when some 38 centimetres of rain falls. I used to try to trap as much of this rain-water as I could in order to irrigate my crops until the next major supply of water came in March of the following year. This was when the Himalayan snows started to melt and caused the rivers to swell. Not having a regular supply of rain throughout the year meant that my work was made that much more difficult."

Peter: "I must be going in a few minutes, but could you tell me a little about schools in Pakistan before I leave?"

Mr Hussein: "There are all types of education in Pakistan—primary and secondary schools, colleges and universities. Some schools were opened by missionaries, but most are now run by the Government."

Peter: "What languages are taught in the schools of Rawalpindi?"

Idris: "I think I can answer this, seeing that I went to a school in Rawalpindi when I last visited Pakistan. The short answer to your question is many. The teachers teach in Urdu, but all the children have to learn English. That's compulsory. After that, there are many optional languages taught, especially in secondary schools. These include Arabic, Persian, Punjabi, French, German and many others."

Peter looked at his watch and realised that he had kept Mr Hussein and Idris talking for over an hour. He also thought that his mother might now be wondering where he had got to after school. So he thanked Mr Hussein and Idris for answering his questions so interestingly. Mr Hussein and Idris said that they too had enjoyed their chat and that perhaps Peter would like to call again some time.

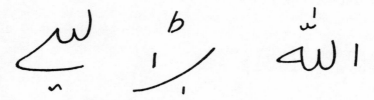

Example of Urdu writing

SUGGESTIONS FOR FURTHER STUDY

1   Try and find out to which countries, excluding Britain, Muslims have emigrated in search of a higher standard of living.

2   Imagine you were emigrating with your family. What difficulties do you think you would face? How would you try to overcome them?

3   Find out the history of the Punjab. Draw a map to help you. What other main religion is to be found there? Find out as much as you can about that religion.

4   How does the climate of a country affect the way the inhabitants live? Consider both a hot and a cold country. Would you describe Britain as a hot or cold country?

5   Collect as much information as you can about life in Britain and Pakistan under the following headings: climate, industry, education, dress, religion, houses, transport, schools, hospitals, diet. Compile a scrap-book with what you have collected. Describe the main differences between the two countries, based on what you have found out.

4 The Prophet Muhammad and the Religion of Islam

Peter and Idris were walking home together after their games lesson and Peter was anxious to know more about Idris's beliefs, because their teacher had begun to explain them in the R.E. lesson that morning. Some of their class-mates had laughed at the teacher's description of what a Muslim wears to pray, and as Peter didn't want to be made fun of he hadn't asked any questions. Now, however, he had just the opportunity to ask a practising Muslim about his religion.

Peter: "Do you mind if I ask you some questions about your religion? I won't if you're not supposed to talk about it."

Idris: "No, that's O.K., Peter. Actually we're allowed to talk about it. In fact, we have a duty to tell anyone who is interested as much as we can. But I don't say much about my beliefs because some people laugh at me and others don't want to listen anyway. And the last thing I want to do is to upset someone over my religion. Anyway, go ahead. What did you want to know?"

Peter: "Well, what I didn't quite understand today was why you are called Muslims. In my religion we call

21

ourselves Christians because we follow the teachings of Jesus Christ, but although you follow the teachings of **Muhammad**, you don't call yourselves Muhammadans. Why not?''

Idris: ''You're quite right about that. In fact, some Muslims get very angry when they are called Muhammadans. I don't, because I know people call us that out of ignorance and they don't mean any harm by it. My dad says that a lot of the books written about Muslims in the past always called us Muhammadans and it is a very old Western way of thinking about us, but I don't think many writers use the word these days.

''The reason we are not called after Muhammad is that we think of Muhammad in a different way from how you think of Jesus. To you Christians, Jesus, as well as having been a man, is part of God. You call him the Son of God sometimes, don't you? So when you worship Jesus you are worshipping God. The reason we are not named after Muhammad is that, when we worship, we can only worship **Allah**. Allah is our only Lord. Muhammad was a great man, but we do not believe he was the Son of God. In fact, we believe that God is one, and therefore he can't be divided up into parts.''

Peter: ''Yes, I think I follow that all right, but it only explains why you're not called Muhammadans. It doesn't tell me why you're called Muslims.''

Idris: ''Well, the word Muslim means someone who submits. You sometimes hear that word in wrestling on TV, don't you? It's when you give in completely to somebody who has power over you. The name of our religion, **Islam**, means to submit to the will of God—or Allah, as we say.''

Peter: ''Let's get back to Muhammad now. What is so important about him if he was only a man and not divine?''

Idris: ''A very good question, Peter, and I'm not sure I can answer it. But we've nearly reached my house now, so why don't you come in and I'll ask my dad to tell you the

22

story of our Prophet Muhammad. He won't mind at all because he was on the early shift from 6 a.m. to 2 p.m., so he's had a rest since finishing work."

Peter had told his mother that if he were late home from school some day he would probably be at Idris's house, so he did not have to worry about her.

When the two boys had sat down inside the house Idris asked his father if he would tell Peter about the Prophet of Islam. Mr Hussein was having a sleep in the chair but he didn't seem to mind being woken up, and the three of them went into the front room so they would not be disturbed by Mrs Hussein and Fatima, who were starting to make tea.

Mr Hussein: "I'll tell you the story of our Prophet, Peter, but if there are any words you don't understand, just interrupt and ask any questions you like. That goes for you too, Idris, because you don't know this story as well as you should.

"Muhammad was born in the year A.D. 570.* That is according to your calendar, Peter, but we have a different way of measuring time. Anyway, for now I'll get on with the story.

"He was born in the city of Mecca, which is in a country now called Saudi Arabia. Saudi Arabia is very hot and much of it is desert. Today it is one of the richest countries in the world because of the oil that has been found there. In Muhammad's lifetime, it was an area where most of the people lived in tribes, moving around the land with their animals and trying to find grazing wherever they could. The name we normally give to such people is nomads, and in this case they had the particular name of **bedouin**. There are still bedouin living like this today.

"Muhammad did not spend his childhood with his parents. His father, Abdullah, died before the boy was born and his mother, Amina, died when he was only six.

*You can learn more about the calendar in Chapter 7.

23

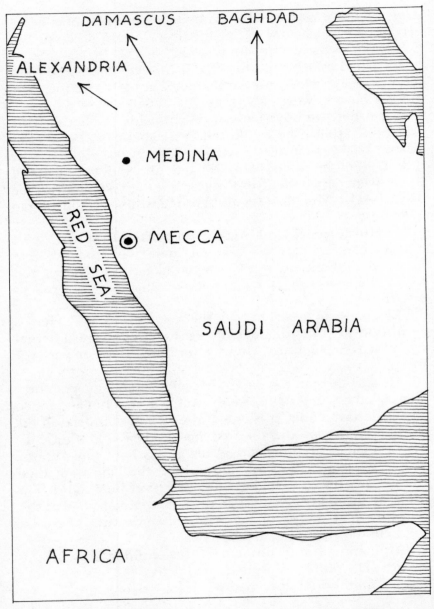

Map of Saudi Arabia showing Mecca and Medina

"At the age of eight, Muhammad's uncle, Abu Talib, became his guardian and proved to be a great help to Muhammad when others attacked him for his beliefs.

"In those days the people of Arabia worshipped many gods. Some towns had a special god of their own, but most of the people would be described as **polytheistic**—that is, they worshipped more than one god.

"As a young man, Muhammad came into contact with these different gods and was brought up to accept the religion of Arabia as his own.

"When the time came to find work, Muhammad became the agent of a woman called **Khadijah**. She was quite wealthy and traded as a merchant, sending caravans from

Muhammad earned his living as a trader dealing with camel trains like this one

Mecca to other cities in the Arab world. Muhammad visited Syria on one occasion, acting as Khadijah's agent, and she was so pleased with the way he carried out his work that she suggested they should marry. Muhammad agreed and, at the age of twenty-five, he married the forty-year-old Khadijah.

"On his travels Muhammad came into contact with many other religious groups in addition to the ones he had known from childhood. He met Jews, Christians and probably Zoroastrians (the old religion of the Persian Empire). Up to the age of forty, he would have been both interested in, and concerned with, the beliefs and practices of these different groups.

"However, at the age of forty, Muhammad began to have visions of the Angel Gabriel. These first visions appeared to him on a hill at Hira, a little way from Mecca, a place where he used to go for the peace and quiet that helped him to think.

"Muhammad heard from Gabriel that he was to be the 'Messenger of God' and he was ordered to 'recite' the words of God he was receiving. This command to recite is the meaning of the word **Qur'an**—the name of the Holy Book of the Muslims.

"Muhammad experienced a great deal of hostility from many of the Meccans. In fact, both he and his fellow-believers had to leave the city. Some went to Abyssinia, but eventually the whole group of Muslims became established in a town in Arabia called Medina.

"It took time, wars and negotiation before the religion of Islam became accepted by the Meccans, but in A.D. 630 Islam was established as the dominant religion in the region and Muhammad became the overall leader of the Meccans.

"The Prophet died in 632, soon after his triumph on entering Mecca. The Muslims had as their new leader a man called Abu Bakr, who was the first **caliph**, which means successor.

"Although Abu Bakr was the leader of the Muslims, he

Muhammad teaching

was not a complete successor to Muhammad. Muhammad had been both a religious and social leader as well as a prophet. Abu Bakr was not a prophet.

"The death of Muhammad meant that the messages from God were at an end and the Holy Book of Islam, the Qur'an, was therefore completed. All that is to be found in it was recited by Muhammad over a period of about twenty years and, because of this, the Qur'an is very different from the Holy Books of most other religions. The religious books of

Christians and Jews are collections of writings made over long periods and produced by many different people. The Holy Book of the Sikhs is also a collection, though compiled over a shorter period, and the Hindus do not have one sacred book but a number, again produced by different people at different times.

"In the period following the death of Muhammad, the religion of Islam spread rapidly. The new religion was not always accepted by the people of North Africa, but the Arab armies that led the spread of Islam were far superior to any other powers in that part of the world and they soon controlled land from as far west as Algeria to as far east as Persia.

"The Islamic world today is far larger than in the days of Muhammad and the first caliph, but it might have been even larger but for a battle in France which was won by the French leader Charles Martel.

"At one time Muslim armies controlled a large part of Europe, including Spain, southern France, parts of Italy and Eastern Europe. It looked for a while as if these armies were unbeatable and would conquer the whole of Europe and convert the population to Islam. Although most of the fine mosques and palaces built by the Muslims at this time have been destroyed or damaged in some way, some can still be visited in Spain. These are among the most beautiful buildings in that country.

"Just how many people in the world are Muslims is impossible to say because there are many millions in Russia and China, and we do not have accurate figures from these countries. Today Islam is the religion which is gaining most converts in Africa.

"Most of the Muslims who live here in Britain come from Pakistan, India and Bangladesh, but some come from Nigeria and North Africa and others from Uganda, Kenya and Tanzania."

Peter: "Is there still a caliph who leads all the world's Muslims today?"

Mr Hussein: "No. In fact, the Islamic world was only really united under a caliph for about thirty years. The first caliph, Abu Bakr, was the leader for two years, from 632 to 634. He was followed by Umar, from 634 to 644. Then came Uthman, from 644 to 656, and Ali, from 656 to 661.

"These four caliphs were chosen by the community. It was believed that the leader of the Muslims should be chosen and not be the leader just because of his birth. The caliph Umar actually ordered that his son should not be allowed to succeed him as caliph.

"The first four caliphs are known as the **Rashidun** (the orthodox). After these four the caliphate did become hereditary, and the capital of the Islamic world moved regularly as different families gained control of the caliphate."

Peter: "In all the time that has passed since the lifetime of Muhammad, how has the one short book, the Qur'an, managed to provide Muslims with all the rules and regulations they need in their lives?"

Mr Hussein: "The short answer to that, Peter, is that it hasn't. Muslims regard the Qur'an as the word of Allah and therefore something to be obeyed, but it was soon clear that there were problems facing Muslims that Muhammad had not dealt with in his recitations. So, we have other writings which help us to know what is right and what is wrong."

Peter: "Who was the author of these other writings? It couldn't have been Muhammad, could it?"

Mr Hussein: "No, it wasn't Muhammad who wrote them down, but a lot of our laws are based on what Muhammad said during his lifetime. He often had to settle disputes and make decisions, and from what he said on such occasions, general rules could be established.

"When he had died, people who had known him made a special effort to remember his advice and rulings on particular problems. All these sayings, **Hadith**, of the Prophet were collected and written down so that they would always be available for people to consult.

29

"Later too, law books were written which dealt with questions and problems that the Prophet had never mentioned. These books were based on decisions made by representatives of the whole religious community. They tried to reach decisions which they thought the Prophet himself might have reached.

"Most of the questions of religion, and indeed life, are covered in these three sources, but only the Qur'an is the word of Allah.

"And now, Peter, before we have any more of your questions, we shall have a cup of tea, because all this talking is making my mouth dry."

5 The Pillars of Islam

Peter was eager to ask more questions, for his curiosity had been aroused further by what Mr Hussein had said. As soon as they had finished drinking their tea he took the opportunity to bring the conversation back to the subject of what Muslims actually do when they submit to Allah.

Mr Hussein decided Idris ought to answer, and so he replied to Peter's questions.

Idris: "To begin with, Peter, every Muslim must make a statement about his beliefs. I suppose the nearest thing to it in Christianity is the creed which members of the different Christian Churches recite. The word creed comes from a word that means 'I believe', and when we make our statement of belief we call it the **Shahada**. The Shahada must always be spoken in Arabic, the language of the Qur'an."

Idris stood up and recited the Shahada for Peter:

"Laa-ilaaha il-lal-lah ; Muhammad rasu-lul-laah."

Peter: "You'll have to tell me what it means, you know."

Idris: "I know that, I just thought you ought to hear it as we say it. It means, 'There is no god but God, Muhammad is the Prophet of God'. In fact, Peter, we have many prophets in Islam besides Muhammad. In our religion Jesus too is a prophet, but we Muslims do not believe he was the Son of God. We also believe in the prophets who appear in what you call the Old Testament. We trace our religion back through men like Elisha, Moses, Abraham, and others. We regard them as messengers who brought the word from Allah. Allah has sent many prophets in history, but each time the messages brought by the prophets have been

31

misunderstood by the people who heard them. It was only when Muhammad delivered the message that it was understood by man. That is why we call Muhammad the 'Seal of the Prophets'—the last of the prophets.

"When we recite the Shahada we are saying that we know there is only one God and that we know what he wants us to do because we recognise Muhammad as his messenger.

"Muhammad received the Qur'an directly from Allah and passed the message on for all men to hear and understand. It is the Qur'an which helps us to know what Allah wants us to do.

"The recitation of the Shahada is only one of the five important acts all Muslims must perform, but by making this declaration of faith a man takes the first important step towards becoming a Muslim.

"The five important acts I mentioned are called the five pillars of Islam. They are the foundation on which Islam is built.

"The second of the pillars is prayer. When we pray we call it performing a **salat**. You can come to the mosque with me some time and I will show you all the men and boys praying together. It is important for Muslims to pray together because Islam is a religion which places great emphasis on men acting as brothers. When we pray we try to do so in groups, particularly at special festivals and on Fridays, which is the day we should try to attend a special prayer whenever possible."

Peter: "Why did you say I can see the men and boys at the mosque? Why not Fatima and your mother? I've seen Fatima waiting for the van to take her to the mosque after school."

Idris: "Fatima does attend the mosque for her lessons, but my mother does not go there regularly. When Fatima reaches the age of twelve she too will not attend the mosque very often. By that age she will be regarded as a young woman rather than a girl, and women do not attend the

32

mosques as often as men. When they do attend, however, they usually go into a different room from the men. At some mosques I have been to, the women have worshipped in a separate gallery and even used a different entrance from the men. This is done so that Muslims will not be distracted in any way as they recite their prayers. On the other hand, there are other mosques in Britain where women do pray in the same room as men. Practice here tends to vary. Whatever arrangements are made for women at mosques, they normally say their prayers at home, either together or alone. They perform all the actions which you will see in the mosque, but they do it here in the house instead.

"My mother, and most of the Muslim women around here, teach their young children how to pray so that when they are old enough to attend the mosque they will know what to do.

"The third pillar is a tax which we must pay annually, the **zakat** tax. This is a kind of charitable donation given to the poor. In the early days of Islam it was collected by the authorities and distributed to the poor among the faithful. It was also used to equip the soldiers in the army in order that they might gain victory in their holy wars.

"These days the zakat is not collected, and instead we pay it directly to the poor. Every Muslim must give a fortieth part of his savings to the poor. The money is usually paid before the end of the month of **Ramadan**."

Mr Hussein: "We do not consider anyone in Britain to be truly poor so we send the zakat money to poor people in India and Pakistan. We believe that by giving $2\frac{1}{2}$ per cent of our savings to the poor we shall have the remaining $97\frac{1}{2}$ per cent blessed by Allah. We also know that after death we shall obtain a great reward in paradise."

Idris: "The fourth pillar is **Sawm**. Most religions seem to include a period in the year when people go without food for a time. I know some Hindu girls who spend a week praying for a good husband, and they fast during the day for the whole of that week. The old lady next door never eats

33

or drinks on Sunday until she has been to Holy Communion at church."

Peter: "Yes, I've come across things like that. I know some Roman Catholics who don't eat meat on Fridays. Ian Kelly always gets a butter pie for dinner on Friday instead of his usual meat and potato pie. I think at one time Christians in Europe used to fast right through Lent, although these days people just give up sweets or cakes or something like that."

Idris: "When we fast it is for a whole month, and it can prove very uncomfortable. On the twenty-ninth or thirtieth of **Shahban**, that is the eighth month of our year, we begin our fast. It lasts for the whole of the month of Ramadan and we know from the Qur'an that we should fast at this time:

> 'The month of Ramadan in which was revealed the Qur'an . . . and whosoever of you is present, let him fast this month.' (Surah 2, verse 185)

"We are not allowed to swallow anything at all during the hours of daylight. You can imagine that by evening we are really thirsty and hungry, especially those men who have been working hard in a hot factory all day.

"Ramadan comes at a different time each year because we have a different calendar from you in the West. It is possible for Ramadan to fall in December and, some years later, in July. You can see that when it falls in summer it is much more difficult to follow the demands of fasting than when it falls in winter—the days are so much longer and the heat so much greater."

Peter: "Does everyone fast?"

Idris: "No, not everyone. Old and sick people do not have to fast, but if the sick recover they should do so at a later date. Pregnant women need not fast, nor do young children, but by the time you reach my age you are expected to do so. I have fasted each year since I was ten, and some

34

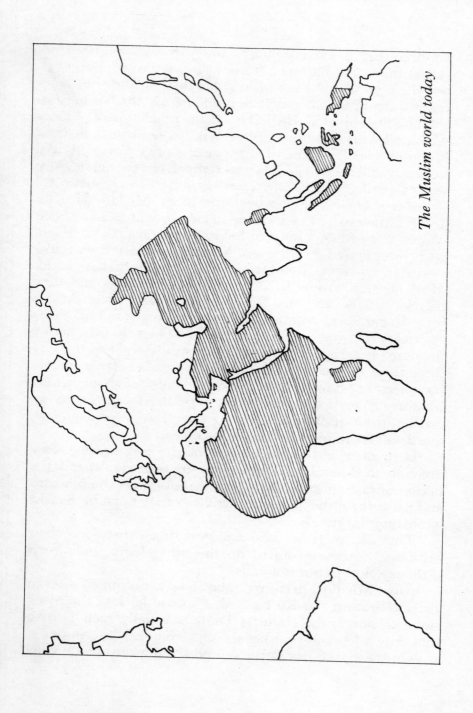

The Muslim world today

children begin even younger than that. It varies from family to family. Fatima has not begun to fast properly yet, but she goes without her meal at lunch-time and she sometimes waits until it is nearly bedtime before she has her tea.

"The fifth pillar is **Hajj**. This is the pilgrimage to Mecca which all Muslims must try to make at least once in their lifetimes. I shall go when I am sixteen—my family will need to save up till then in order to send me. Even though it's two years away I get quite excited every time I think about it."

Peter: "Have you ever been to Mecca, Mr Hussein?"

Mr Hussein: "Yes indeed, Peter. In fact, I have been twice—once when I lived in Pakistan and again a couple of years after arriving in Britain. My wife has also been once.

"Pilgrims travel to Mecca from all around the world. Most of those from Britain fly to Saudi Arabia and then travel into Mecca by bus. Other pilgrims reach Saudi Arabia by boat, car, lorry and bus, and some even go on foot. Years ago many pilgrims would leave for Mecca six months before the date of the pilgrimage, and they would walk all the way there from thousands of kilometres away. The great routes for pilgrims have many graves alongside them where Muslims have died in their effort to reach Mecca. Today we can get there quite quickly by air and, as a consequence, more and more pilgrims arrive each year.

"Both men and women perform the pilgrimage, some arriving in Mecca a month early in order to spend the period of fasting in the holy city. Guides meet the pilgrims and show them the necessary activities they must undertake while on pilgrimage.

"The male pilgrims wear seamless sheets instead of their ordinary clothes. Women, on the other hand, may wear ordinary clothes but not veils.

"Most Muslims perform an optional act of making seven circuits around the **Ka'ba** and, if possible, kiss the black stone on one of the circuits. There is usually such a crush that only a few pilgrims get the chance to kiss the stone.

"On the eighth day of the month the pilgrims go to Mina

36

The Ka'ba

(about 5 kilometres from Mecca) and there they rest until the morning of the ninth, when they proceed to Arafat. A little before sunset the pilgrims hurry to Muzdalifa, where two salats are performed. The night is spent here and the following morning pilgrims return to Mina, collecting pebbles as they go. Seven pebbles are thrown at a **jamra** (a pile of stones encircled by a pillar or wall). There are three jamras in all, one is stoned on the tenth day and the other two on the eleventh and twelfth respectively.

"These piles of stones represent Satan to the pilgrim, and they re-enact the stoning of Satan by Abraham.

"The sacrifice of an animal (usually a sheep or goat) is now performed. This sacrifice commemorates the time when Abraham was prepared to sacrifice his own son. Some pilgrims prepare for this act personally while others prefer to enlist the help of a butcher. Following the sacrifice, the men have their heads shaved or closely cropped and the women cut off at least $2\frac{1}{2}$ centimetres of hair.

"The pilgrims then return to Mecca, where the Ka'ba is again circled seven times, after which prayer is performed.

"Water is now drunk from the **Zamzam** well, the sacred well of Mecca. This well, according to Muslim belief, was opened up by Gabriel to provide water for Hagar and Ishmael—the wife and son of Abraham. The drinking of the water is followed by the re-enactment of the plight of Hagar. When she could not find any water to drink, Hagar ran backwards and forwards between two small hills, Marwa and Safa. The pilgrims run seven times between these two hills.

"The night of the eleventh is spent at Mina. On the twelfth the pilgrims return to Mecca and usually perform a final series of seven circuits of the Ka'ba.

"Some pilgrims then leave for home, but most visit the Prophet's tomb at Medina before leaving Saudi Arabia.

"All the pillars have one thing in common, Peter. They draw people closer together as Muslims. No matter how rich or how poor a Muslim, he must still perform the duties set out in the five pillars. Having made their statement of belief, all men stand shoulder to shoulder in the salat, all must fast during the month of Ramadan, the rich must remember the needs of the poor in paying the zakat, and at the Hajj Muslims of all colours, from every part of the world, speaking a variety of languages, join together in simple dress and are equal before Allah.

"Islam tries to be a religion where differences in wealth, power, language, colour and background can be overcome by the common experience of the five pillars.

"Now it's getting late, Peter. Have you any more questions before you go?"

Peter: "There's one question I must ask. When you quoted from the Qur'an you mentioned a word I did not understand—**surah**, I think it was."

Idris: "This is simply the way the Qur'an is divided up. The Bible is divided into books under different headings, like Genesis, Exodus, Acts, Romans and many others. The Qur'an too is divided, each section having a name and a number. The first section is called 'The Opening' and is surah 1. The second section is titled 'The Cow' and is surah 2. The nearest equivalent to it is a chapter in a book. Each of the thirty surahs is divided into verses, just like a chapter in the Bible."

Peter left Idris's house with his questions answered, but he realised that there was still a lot more for him to learn about Islam.

6 Festivals

All religions have special occasions which are times for celebration and rejoicing. In Britain the major festivals connected with Christianity are also public holidays. At Christmas and Easter Christians celebrate the birth and resurrection of Jesus, and in doing so everyone tries to enjoy himself. People send each other cards and try to be friendly towards one another.

The Hussein family also celebrate special festivals, but in their case these mark Islamic rather than Christian events.

Idris often jokes with Peter about the festivals because the Husseins have been in Britain for some years and they have begun to follow the British way of life in a number of their activities. At Christmas, for instance, Idris and Fatima go to bed on Christmas Eve and awake the morning after to find presents, as well as chocolates and fruit in their bedroom. They exchange Christmas cards with friends at school, and they attend Christmas parties both at school and at Mr Hussein's factory. Last year Idris went to a couple of parties in friends' homes, including one at Peter's.

At Easter the children have a good selection of chocolate eggs, and the whole family spend Easter Monday in the local park rolling their eggs down the hill. Fatima enjoys this, but Idris usually manages to find a game of football to join in. Egg rolling is carried on by thousands of people in Preston every Easter Monday, and the Husseins join in maintaining this ancient tradition, along with Hindus, Sikhs and Christians.

The aspect of all this that so amuses Idris and Fatima is

that they celebrate at the British festivals and then at the Muslim ones too. It also means that they manage a few extra days holiday from school when the major festivals fall in term time. That is enough to make Peter more than a little envious.

When Peter questioned Mr Hussein and Idris about the beliefs of Muslims he learned about the five pillars of Islam. He now discovered that the major festivals of Islam are closely connected with two of the pillars.

In most religions a period of self-denial, usually by fasting, is followed by a period of celebration. Islam is no exception to this rule. The month of Ramadan is a period when many people make the great effort of fasting during the hours of daylight, and the end of the fast is eagerly anticipated by all who have participated in it.

The Arabic word for a festival is **Id**. There are two important Ids in the Islamic year. One of these is the **Id al Fitr**, although sometimes Muslim children do not know it by its full name—Fatima, for instance, calls it simply Id. Id al Fitr takes place on the first of **Shawal**, the month which follows Ramadan.

On the morning of Id al Fitr the Husseins get up early, but Mr Hussein does not leave for work, nor do the children prepare for school. Mr Hussein's employer has more than 50 per cent of his work-force who are practising Muslims so he arranges for the first day of Shawal to be taken as a holiday. In doing this he can change his production plans well in advance and is not faced with absenteeism.

The schools which Idris and Fatima attend also know of this Id, as Mr Hussein and many other Muslim parents have written to the headteachers to inform them that their children will be absent on that day.

Everyone in the family takes a bath in the morning so that they are ready to perform the special salat which marks the end of Ramadan. Mr Hussein and Idris then leave the house and drive across the town to a large car-park.

In some towns in Britain, and in many parts of the

41

Muslim world, worshippers gather in the largest mosque in the area and celebrate the first of Shawal. In parts of India and Pakistan the salat takes place in the open air, and the Muslims who attend Mr Hussein's mosque continue that tradition by meeting on one of the large municipal car-parks.

When Mr Hussein and Idris arrive they find there are already more than 3000 worshippers gathered. It is a deeply moving moment for both of the Husseins as they stand shoulder to shoulder with thousands of fellow-Muslims and perform a salat.

As the salat ends the worshippers greet each other and exchange best wishes and embraces. The men drift off in groups and the celebrations begin. Everyone wears his best clothes and many have gifts in their cars. Three other cars follow Mr Hussein's back to his house, and when Idris and Mr Hussein go inside they find that three Muslim families are already there. When the men from the three cars arrive there is a house full of happy, smiling faces.

As each guest arrives he or she is greeted with best wishes and embraces and each adult distributes presents to all the children in the house. Mostly the children receive money, but a few receive toys and books. Idris and Fatima have done rather well out of the proceedings, both having received over £12, with the promise of more to come in the evening when they visit neighbours and friends.

Mrs Hussein has been busy in the kitchen since performing her salat at home, and Fatima has seen to the laying of the table and has washed up the pans for her mother.

When everyone has arrived and all the presents have been given, Mrs Hussein serves up a splendid dinner. It tastes even better, as it is the first meal eaten at midday for over a month.

On the sideboard and window-sills there are a number of greetings cards, which are a further example of how Id is similar to Christmas.

Most of the Id cards are written in Urdu, but some are in English. Some have arrived from Pakistan, but the majority

42

Id cards

have come from friends in Britain. Id cards can be bought at many shops in most large towns where Muslims live. Those that are printed in Britain sometimes have views of British cities on the front. The Husseins have sent over fifty cards to friends and relatives all around the world.

Mr Hussein has already sent some money to Pakistan to be used to help the poor, but some of his friends had forgotten to do so. Id al Fitr is the last day to do this, and so two of the guests leave early to visit the post office and send some money to their home villages.

Soon after all the guests have left, the Husseins put on their coats, collect a few parcels for distribution to other friends, and then all get into the car. They do not leave for their friends' homes at once, however, but drive instead to the local cemetery. It is a custom to visit the graves of dead relatives on the first of Shawal and, as Mr Hussein has a cousin buried in the local cemetery, the family need to visit the grave and say a short prayer. There are many other Muslim families there and many more will come before the day is over.

The evening is spent visiting friends, exchanging greetings as well as presents and finally, late at night, the family returns home and to bed, very tired and very full.

The festival of Id al Fitr is the most important day of celebration for the majority of Muslims, but it is officially called the "minor" festival.

The "major" festival is not celebrated with the same vigour, but it is still a day when Idris and Fatima miss school and when some presents are given to the children. The major festival is called **Id al Adha** and is celebrated on the tenth day of the last month in the Islamic year, **Dhu-al-Hijah**.

The Hajj (pilgrimage) takes place during this month. Those Muslims who go on the pilgrimage commemorate the time when Abraham was prepared to sacrifice his own son.

Those Muslims who have not joined in the Hajj nevertheless join in the celebration of the sacrifice. A special salat is performed, which in some areas will again be in the open air, but which Mr Hussein will perform in his mosque.

Mr Hussein has joined together with six other men and purchased a cow. The seven men visit the abattoir on the tenth of Dhu-al-Hijah, and they pray while the animal has its throat cut in the way prescribed by Islamic law. Other Muslims are also at the abattoir, some singly with a sheep or a goat, others in groups of seven with a cow.

Mr Hussein's share of the cow is prepared by Mrs Hussein, and a number of friends come along again to join in the meal.

Last year some of the men who worship at the same mosque as Mr Hussein were taken to court for sacrificing a goat in their backyard without stunning it first. They had not been in Britain long and were unaware of the facilities at

44

the abattoir. Mr Hussein found the whole incident very embarrassing and everyone hoped nothing like that would happen this year.

Many of the Muslims do not buy an animal to sacrifice, but instead send money to their home villages so that a goat can be bought and sacrificed there and the meat distributed among the poor. Sending money to Pakistan or India, then, is another way of performing the sacrifice and benefiting the poor.

Id al Fitr and Id al Adha are the two chief festivals of the Islamic year. Peter asked Mr Hussein whether the tenth of **Muharram** was celebrated, as he had read in a school textbook that it was an important day for Muslims. Mr Hussein explained that this day was not celebrated by many of the Muslims who come from India and Pakistan. It is chiefly celebrated by a section of Muslims known as the Shi'a, who live mainly in Iran. He added that some celebrations take place on the twelfth of **Rabi-al-Auwal**, the birthday of the Prophet. The main event on this occasion is the reading of some Islamic history in the mosque with the addition of a sermon if a guest speaker is visiting the area.

7 The Muslim Calendar

Peter was interested by something he noticed in a photograph at the Husseins' home. It showed a newly built mosque in Britain. Peter was particularly curious about the two sets of numbers which could be seen on one of the mosque's walls. The name of the mosque was clearly shown and beneath it was the date A.D. 1974. Alongside this number was a different set of figures: A.H. 1394.

The Islamic world, like many civilisations, has its own way of reckoning time. In the past, Western Europe has had a number of different calendars, but the one we use today divides the whole history of the world into two eras. The division between these eras occurs with the life of Jesus of Nazareth. We always refer to events which happened before the birth of Jesus as occurring at a date B.C. (before Christ), while events occurring since are said to be in the year A.D. (*anno Domini*—in the year of our Lord). It is obvious from the meanings of B.C. and A.D. that this dating is based on a Christian view of the world.

This system has become common in parts of the world where the culture is non-Christian mainly because European countries, which are predominantly Christian, used to have great empires which covered much of the world.

Today, Western society is the major industrial area of the world, and developing countries which attempt to become more like the West adopt a number of Western practices, including the dating system used by the great trading nations of the world.

Some non-Christians prefer to date events according to a dual system, using the Gregorian calendar of the West (named after Pope Gregory XIII, who instituted it) and another calendar based on different criteria. The Muslim world has its own system of dating.

When Peter had asked about the history of the religion, he was told that Muhammad had to leave Mecca and move to the town of Medina. The move to Medina is usually referred to as "the flight from Mecca", but in fact those families who believed the message brought by Muhammad considered that he moved to Medina in a carefully planned emigration. The word Muslims use for this move is **Hijra**.

At the Hijra Muhammad abandoned his own tribe in Mecca and sought a new base in Medina (then called Yathrib). He arrived there on September 20th A.D. 622.

No new calendar was introduced then, but within a few years there was a real need for one. In the period when Umar was the caliph the Muslim authorities were having difficulties because the letters and orders sent out by him had no date on them. Umar decided to find out what the other great empires did, and he discovered that the Greeks and the Persians dated all their letters according to an era. Umar therefore determined that the Islamic Empire should also date events according to its own era, but it was necessary to decide which event should mark the beginning of that era.

Some advisers suggested that it ought to be the date of Muhammad's birth, but Umar rejected the idea because there was no certainty as to the exact date. Instead he ordered that the emigration from Mecca to Medina should be regarded as the starting-point of the Muslim era, and the year of the Hijra was therefore the first year in the Islamic calendar. This decision was only arrived at in the year A.H. (*anno Hijra*) 17.

The actual day of the Hijra was not to be counted as the first day of A.H. 1 because the months of the year had already been established in the Qur'an. The Islamic era

47

therefore began on the first day of the month of Muharram in the year of the Hijra. This was July 16th A.D. 622. It was also 933 in the Seleucid era, one of the major dating systems with which Muslims came into contact at the time.

MEASUREMENT OF MONTHS

"He [Allah] it is who appointed the sun a splendour and the moon a light, *and measured for her stages, that ye might know the number of years,* and the reckoning." (Surah 10, verse 6)

These words from the Qur'an tell us that the months and years are to be measured according to the stages of the moon. Such a method of measuring time is usually known as a system of reckoning by lunar months. Twelve of these pure lunar months are termed a lunar year.

The lunar year is not the same length as a solar year. (A solar year is the time taken for the Earth to pass around the sun: it is on a variation of this that the Western calendar is based, adding an extra day each four years to provide a neat sequence.) The lunar year lasts only 354 days, and so each year the Islamic calendar falls eleven days behind the Western calendar. Thirty-three lunar years take about as long as thirty-two solar years.

Traditionally, the beginning of the month, and indeed of the year, is only established by an actual sighting of the new moon. It will be obvious from this that a day does not begin at twelve midnight but at sunset. Islamic days run from sunset to sunset, hence a new month can begin whenever the new moon is sighted, even if this is nine o'clock at night.

The Islamic tradition of the month commencing with the sighting of the new moon is upheld in Britain. It is not always easy to see the moon, however, owing to the low cloud cover that is often in evidence. The Muslim world operates an early warning system to deal with just such problems.

Muslims in countries where the moon is more easily seen report the first sighting and the news is relayed by government departments to embassies in cities around the world.

In Britain the Algerian, Moroccan or Tunisian Embassy is usually the first to hear and informs the Association of Imams that the moon has been sighted. The various Muslim communities can ring the Association of Imams and hear about the new moon being seen. The word is then passed around the community and everyone knows that a new month has begun.

This activity is not necessary every month, but it is important for the first day of Ramadan and the first day of Shawal—for on the first day of Ramadan the fast begins and on the first of Shawal it comes to an end.

The Islamic months are as follows:

1 Muharram
2 Safar
3 Rabi-al-Auwal
4 Rabi-al-Thani
5 Jamadi-al-Auwal
6 Jamadi-al-Thani
7 Rajjab
8 Shahban
9 Ramadan
10 Shawal
11 Dhu-al-Qadah
12 Dhu-al-Hijah

The major difference caused by the variation in calendars is in the way Muslim festivals are not seasonal as Christian festivals are.

Christian festivals always occur in the same season each year: Christmas is always in winter, Easter is always in spring. Muslim festivals do not follow this pattern. The

49

eleven days lost each lunar year means that the festivals pass through all the seasons.

As an example of this we can look at the festival of Ramadan. In 1978 the fast began on August 5th. Each year it occurs about eleven days earlier, so that by the middle 1880s the fast will take place in the month of May.

As a result of this Muslims do not associate particular weather conditions with particular events, unlike Christians in Britain who often send Christmas cards depicting a snow-covered landscape.

The changes in the seasons can also affect the difficulties involved in abiding by the rules of a festival. When Ramadan falls in July it is much more difficult to fast from dawn to dusk than if it had fallen in December.

MEASUREMENT OF DAYS

As do Westerners, Muslims have a seven-day week. This was common in Arabia long before the time of Muhammad and was probably introduced into Arabia from Babylonia, or by Jews who settled there.

SUGGESTIONS FOR FURTHER STUDY

1   Here is how to change dates from our calendar into the Islamic calendar:
$$\text{A.H.} = \tfrac{33}{32} (\text{A.D.} - 622)$$
To change the other way we reverse the process:
$$\text{A.D.} = \tfrac{32}{33} (\text{A.H.} + 622).$$
You can select important events in history and convert them from one dating system to another by using this formula.

2   To what extent are the five pillars of Islam—confession of faith, worship, fasting, charity and pilgrimage—important in other religions? You may also wish to consider whether these practices have

been popular in Christianity in the past, even though some may not appear to be important today.

3   Try to discover which of the calendars used around the world is the oldest. Can you suggest reasons why the calendar based on the life of Jesus is the international calendar even in countries where Christianity is hardly known?

4   In times past a sixth pillar of Islam was **Jihad**. Find out as much about this as you can and try to discover why it is no longer regarded as being as important as the other five pillars.

5   On a number of occasions it has been noticeable that the religion of the Jews is similar to that of the Muslims. Try to list the similarities between the two religions and also the matters in which they differ.

8 Mosques in Britain

Mosques in Britain can be categorised into two types: those which have been purpose-built and those which have not.

The Quwwat-ul Islam Mosque, Preston. Note the different dating systems. This photograph forms part of the "Islam in Preston" resource kit for teachers. This kit was developed by the authors and is available on loan from the Curriculum Development Centre, Camden Place, Preston.

EXTERNAL APPEARANCE OF PURPOSE-BUILT MOSQUES IN BRITAIN

The mosque which the Hussein family attend has been purpose-built. It contains certain Islamic architectural features which are common to many British mosques. These are:

1 A dome on the roof A dome serves a dual function in Islamic architecture. First, it is a construction of beauty. To build a beautiful house for the worship of Allah is of prime importance to Muslims. Second, a dome is a feature which distinguishes a building as a mosque. That a mosque is to be easily recognised among other buildings is of the utmost importance in Islamic architecture. It is interesting to note that domes in Britain are often made of fibreglass and then decorated with traditional Islamic emblems.

Islamic dome

Minarets: the tall towers with the small domes are the minarets

2 Minarets These are the vertical towers often situated at the top corners of a mosque and capped with a miniature dome. They serve the same dual function as does the dome (see above). In addition to this, however, in Islamic countries the **muezzin** (prayer-summoner or prayer-crier) climbs up inside their much larger minarets and emerges on to a balcony high up. He then walks round this balcony several times as he calls the faithful to prayer. In this way his voice can be heard in all directions. The muezzin thus serves the same function as do church bells to

54

Christians. The muezzin's cry, called the **azzan**, is always the same right across the Muslim world. It is spoken in Arabic:

> "*Allahu-Akbar*
> *Ash-ahdu-an-la-ilaha-illalah*
> *Ash-hado anna Mohammadan-rasulullah*
> *Hayye-alas-salah*
> *Hayye-alal-falah*
> *Allahu-Akbar.*"

In translation this reads:

"God is the greatest
I bear witness that there is no God but Allah
I bear witness that Muhammad is the messenger of
Allah
Come to prayer
Come to security
God is the greatest."

In the early morning the muezzin often adds, "Prayer is better than sleep". In Islamic countries loudspeakers are often housed in the minarets to make this call more effective.

In the mosque which the Husseins attend, the muezzin recites the azzan from some convenient place inside the mosque, usually from the top of a staircase. This practice, common in Britain, is followed because of the likely objections to the muezzin's cry from non-Muslim families living in the immediate vicinity of British mosques. It follows from this that in Britain no loudspeakers are housed in minarets. In fact, British minarets tend to be smaller than those in Islamic countries because the muezzin is not required to climb into them in order to recite the azzan. This means of course that in Britain, unlike Islamic countries, no one outside the mosque hears the call to prayer.

It can be seen from this how Muslims have adapted one of their religious practices in order to fit into the British way of life.

The Raza Mosque, Preston. Note the Islamic architectural features. This photograph forms part of the "Islam in Preston" kit.

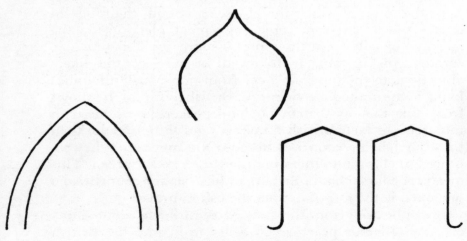

Three types of Islamic arch

3 Arabian arches Many British mosques try to incorporate such arches somewhere. At the mosque which the Husseins attend these can be found above each of the rectangular windows. They have been made with the use of a mould and concrete and then set above the windows for decoration. At other mosques in Britain Arabian arches may have been made with other materials such as wood, fibreglass and the like.

4 A mihrab A **mihrab** is a semicircular alcove which a Muslim faces when engaged in prayer. It is to be found on the Mecca-facing wall in a mosque. In Britain this is the south-eastern wall. This means of course that mosques built east of Mecca will possess mihrabs on their western (Mecca-facing) walls. Mihrabs are often decorated in some prominent way, thus enabling them to be seen easily by a passer-by. The mihrab at the mosque the Husseins attend, for instance, stands out because it is covered with blue mosaic tiles and capped with striking gold paint.

Another feature, which seems to be peculiar to the Husseins' mosque, is that its ground floor is raised nearly a metre above ground level. Five steps lead up to the entrance of this mosque. Although there does not appear to be any religious significance in this characteristic, Mr Hussein values it. The reasoning here is that when praying, Muslims are involved in a more important activity than is the "man in the street". Thus, to be in a higher physical position is commensurate with such an activity.

EXTERNAL APPEARANCE OF NON-PURPOSE-BUILT MOSQUES IN BRITAIN

Mr Hussein told Peter that when he first emigrated to Britain in 1967 there were no purpose-built mosques in Preston, so he used to pray with some other Muslim friends in one of their houses. No alterations were made to the exterior of this terraced house to show that it was being used as a mosque as well as a dwelling-place. Mr Hussein told Peter that some Muslims used to place some Arabic script from the Qur'an above the door or in the window so that others of the same faith would know that prayers were said there. Many Muslims today use houses as mosques, especially where there are few other Muslims living nearby.

Mr Hussein told Peter that, as more Muslims settled in Preston, they needed larger premises for the purpose of prayer than were afforded by the terraced house, and eventually a purpose-built mosque was erected by the local Muslims. Other groups of Muslims in Britain, however, when faced with this same situation, have bought large old buildings (shops, vicarages, churches, etc.) and then modified these for mosque purposes. Where possible, Muslims have tried to add a touch of Islamic architecture to such premises so that the usage of the building can be readily identified. For instance, one might see an artificial dome and minarets above the main doorway of this type of mosque. But generally, non-purpose-built buildings do not lend themselves to touches of Islamic architecture.

INTERNAL APPEARANCE OF PURPOSE-BUILT MOSQUES IN BRITAIN

Idris had invited Peter to the mosque he attends in order to show him what it was like and what Muslims do once they are inside their place of prayer. Peter was excited at the prospect of seeing the inside of a mosque for the first time so he eagerly looked forward to the Saturday afternoon which had been arranged for the visit. Idris had told Peter that the **imam** (priest) at the mosque would be pleased to answer any of his questions.

On entering the mosque, Idris showed Peter the shoe-rack in which the boys placed their shoes.

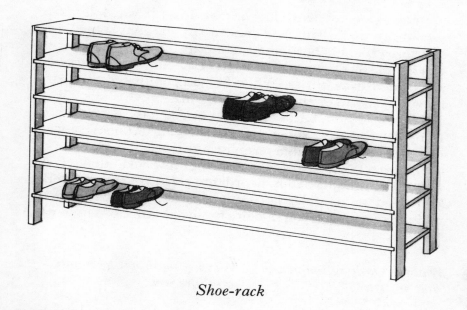

Shoe-rack

Peter: "Why do you take off your shoes when you enter a mosque?"

Idris: "As Muslims we must not defile the house of Allah in any way. If we walked around the mosque with our shoes on we would be treading dirt all around Allah's house. My teacher of Islamic studies told me that the removal of shoes is a custom dating from the second caliph [Umar]."

Idris then went to the imam to tell him that he was here with Peter. After introducing himself to Peter, the imam suggested that they should go around the mosque in the way a Muslim worshipper would when he came to pray. The boys thus went to the cloakroom to take off their coats.

Peter was then taken to the ablution area, where he was shown by Idris exactly how a Muslim washes before going to pray. Idris told Peter that this washing, performed before each time of prayer, was called the **wuzu** and was termed the minor ritual ablution.

Peter watched with interest as Idris washed his face, including his nostrils and mouth (by gargling), his hands and forearms, his head and behind his ears (by rubbing his wet hands over them) and his feet. Each of these actions was performed three times. When he had completed the wuzu, he was ready to enter the prayer-room.

Peter: "I notice that you do not use any bowls or anything like that to collect water for washing. At home, I wash in a washing-up bowl, a basin or a bath."

Imam: "No, we don't use anything like that at the mosque. We believe that, in order to clean yourself properly, you need to use clean, running water, rather than still, dirty water, such as you find in a basin or bath. Consequently,

Wuzu—washing the mouth and nostrils

Wuzu—washing the hands and forearms

wherever possible, we Muslims use running water from taps and showers.''

Peter: "Why do you wash yourselves so carefully before you pray? I usually wash before I dress at home, but I don't do so once I have arrived at church.''

Imam: "Well, Peter, our Prophet taught us to do so. He said:

'O ye who believe, when ye rise up for prayer, wash your faces, and your hands to the elbows and lightly rub your heads and (wash) your feet up to the ankles. . . . Allah would not place a burden on you, but he would purify you. . . . '" (Surah 5, verse 6)

Wuzu—rubbing the head
and behind the ears

Wuzu—washing the feet

Peter: "Do you perform your ablutions if you recite your prayers at home?"

Idris: "Oh yes, we never pray until our bodies are clean."

Peter was impressed when he entered the prayer-room because, while it contained little furniture, it was without doubt a much cared for place.

Idris: "Before we pray we always put a covering on our heads. Muslims usually bring their own prayer-hats to the mosque, but if they forget them they may place any form of covering, such as a handkerchief, on their heads. Muslims cover their heads before they pray as a sign of submission and reverence to Allah."

Peter: "I like the nicely patterned carpet—I think my feet would be cold if there weren't one."

Idris: "Yes, all mosques have a carpet, usually fitted, which acts like a large prayer-mat."

Peter: "What do you mean?"

Prayer-hats

62

Prayer-mat

Idris: "Muslims have to pray observing certain conditions. One of these is that we ought to pray on a prayer-mat. All Muslim families have their own prayer-mats, on which the members of the family pray when they are not in the mosque. Before praying, the worshipper must remember to place the mat facing the **Qibla**. The Qibla is in the direction of the Ka'ba in Mecca. In a mosque this is marked by the mihrab. The fact that the mihrab marks the Qibla has resulted in many mosques not fitting into normal street patterns. Where a rectangular plot of ground has been bought, a mosque will often stand diagonally on it, the mihrab determining the position of the whole building."

Peter: "I understand now—a prayer-mat is a sort of travelling mosque on which Muslims can pray wherever they happen to be. There is no need for individual prayer-mats in the mosque because the carpet acts just like a big prayer-mat."

Idris: "That's right."

Peter: "The mihrab is very different from a Christian altar. It is set into the wall and is empty. The wall where the mihrab is situated is very impressive."

Idris: "Yes, it is called the Qibla wall. By the side of the mihrab is the **minbar**. This is a chair on which the **khatib** (the person reading the Friday sermon) stands as he delivers his sermon. As he speaks he holds his sermon book in one hand and his staff in the other. Thus he is in the same position as our Prophet was when he used to preach."

Peter: "I see, the minbar is a bit like a platform."

Imam: "That's right, Peter. In fact some of the big mosques in Islamic countries do have a platform instead of a minbar like the one we have here."

Peter: "Is the khatib a special person?"

Idris: "That depends. The Friday sermon is usually given by a mosque's imam, but occasionally other notable visiting Muslims (maybe other imams from other mosques in the area) may be invited to act as khatib for the day."

Peter: "What are these incense sticks used for?"

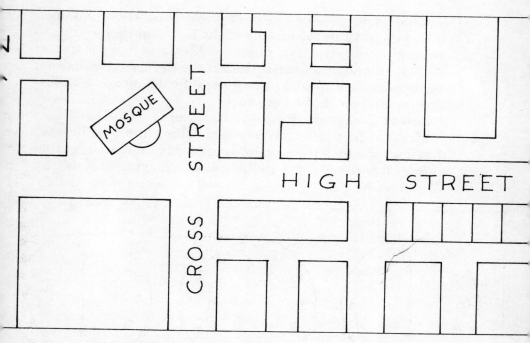

Some mosques differ from surrounding street patterns

Idris: "We call those **agarbattis** and we burn them on Fridays."

Peter: "You've mentioned Fridays a lot. Is that a special day for you?"

Idris: "Yes, it is. We call it a 'day of congregation'."

Imam: "The Qur'an says:

'O ye who believe! When the call is heard for the prayer of the day of congregation, haste unto remembrance of Allah and leave your trading.'" (Surah 62, verse 9)

Idris: "Our Friday is similar to your Christian Sunday or a Jewish Saturday. However, Muslims do not regard Friday as a day of rest—they leave off from work where possible, attend the salat in the middle of the day, and then return to work. Where this is not possible, Muslims make a special effort to attend other salats during the day. They will often try to wear their best clothes for the Friday prayers as well as some non-alcoholic perfume."

Peter: "What are these six clocks for?"

Idris: "That is a prayer-board telling the worshippers the times at which they ought to pray. Muslims are required to pray five times a day. The times, however, vary day by

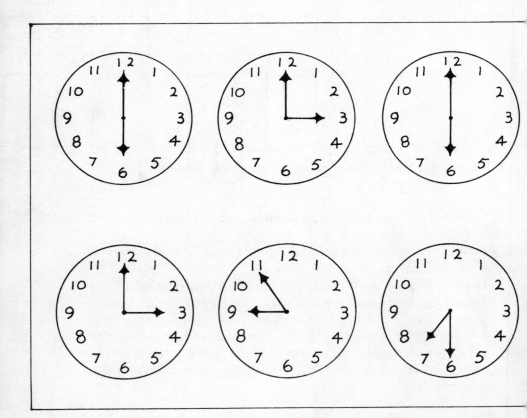

Prayer-board

day as the sun moves. These clocks therefore help the worshippers to know the times for prayer."

Peter: "But what is the sixth clock for?"

Idris: "That tells the worshippers the time of the main Friday salat when the khatib is present."

Imam: "Some prayer-boards contain nine clocks. The extra three tell the worshipper the times of sunrise, noon and sunset. This is because some Muslims believe that they are forbidden to pray ten minutes either side of sunrise and noon, and ten minutes before sunset."

Peter: "The decorations in the mosque are unusual."

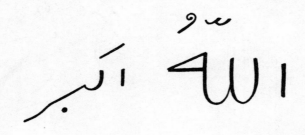

Example of Arabic script

Idris: "Yes, no images, statues or stained glass are allowed in mosques. As a result **calligraphy** or Arabic script is used as a design. Passages of the Qur'an are shown on boards or cloth as decoration. Another decoration Muslims use is geometrical and floral design. You will also notice that much of the mosque is painted in green. Green is the traditional Islamic colour."

Peter: "When is this microphone used?"

Idris: "It's used for large gatherings when the main prayer-room is too small."

67

Peter had been in the mosque for some time now. It would soon be time for the men and boys to come to the mosque to pray. The imam suggested to Idris that he stood at the back of the prayer-room with Peter and explained the positions of prayer to his friend.

In order for a salat to be valid it must be preceded by the **niya**. This is a statement of intent by the worshipper, who states that he intends to perform a particular salat. The worshipper raises his hands to his ears and recites the **takbir**, the magnification of Allah—"Allahu Akbar" (God is the greatest). The right hand is now placed on top of the

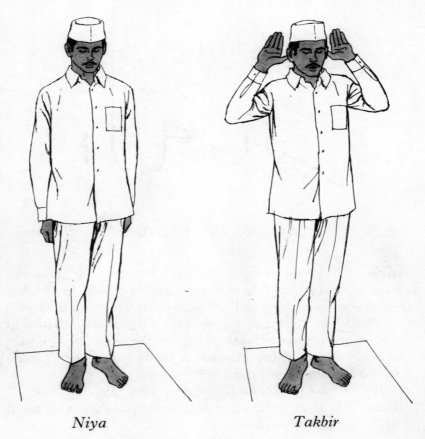

Niya   *Takbir*

left and the two are placed a little above the navel. The
fatiha is now recited:

"Praise be to Allah, Lord of the worlds,
The beneficent, the merciful.
Owner of the Day of Judgement,
Thee (alone) we worship; Thee (alone) we ask for help.

Show us the straight path,
The path of those whom Thou has favoured;
Not (the path) of those who earn thine anger nor of those
who go astray."

Reciting the fatiha

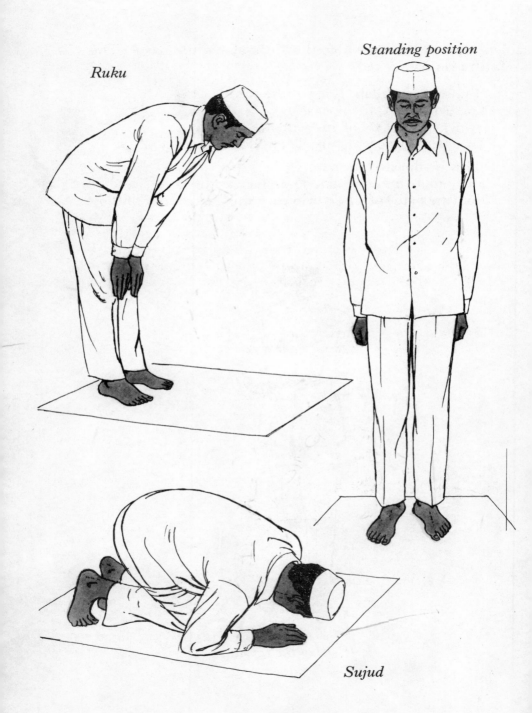

Ruku

Standing position

Sujud

The fatiha has often been compared to the Lord's Prayer in Christianity. It is used on many occasions other than in the salat. A few short verses from the Qur'an follow the fatiha. There follows the **ruku** (bowing). The back is bent until the palms of the hands are level with the knees. In this position the worshipper repeats three times, "All glory to God the Greatest". The worshipper then stands up and recites "Allah heeds him who praises Him, praise be to thee". The worshipper then goes into the **sujud** position (the prostration), with his head placed on the ground. He then takes up a half-kneeling, half-sitting position, which is basically sitting on his haunches. A further prostration then takes place. Women perform slight variations of movement but the procedure is basically the same. From the fatiha to the second prostration one **rak'a** is constituted.

Sitting on the haunches

The number of rak'as in a salat varies according to which salat is being performed:

the salat al fajr (dawn) contains two rak'as
the salat al zuhr (midday) contains four rak'as
the salat al asr (afternoon) contains four rak'as
the salat al maghrib (sunset) contains three rak'as
the salat al isha (evening) contains four rak'as.

The final prostration is followed by the **tashahud** (profession of faith): "There is no god but God; Muhammad is the Prophet of God." The salat ends when the worshipper turns first to his right and then to his left. This is termed the **salam** (salutation). The main Friday prayer consists of two rak'as plus a short sermon lasting some ten minutes.

During a salat some Muslims handle **subhas** (rosaries). These consist of three groups of beads, each group being separated by two larger beads set transversely. There are thirty-three beads within each group, making a total of ninety-nine. The number represents the ninety-nine beautiful names of Allah. It is also used in the counting of prayers by the individual worshipper.

Peter now realised how much Muslims have to learn before they can pray correctly.

Subhas

Although he had heard the word "imam" used on many occasions by Idris and his family, Peter had never had the term explained to him properly. The imam himself was pleased to tell Peter the meaning of the word.

Imam: "An imam is not a priest in the sense that Christians would understand it. He is rather a leader of congregational prayer. Any respected member of the Muslim community may lead such prayer—thus a mosque may have many members, each acting as an imam at certain times. This is what happens at this mosque. In effect, an imam ceases to be an imam when he is not involved in leading congregational prayer.

"However, that is a literal interpretation of the word. As you know, I am often referred to as the imam or priest at this mosque. You will understand from what I have said that I can only possibly be an imam on five occasions a day. That is when I lead the congregational prayers—a task which I mainly, but not always, perform. When I am not leading the prayer I act like a priest—helping and teaching Muslims as much as I can about the Muslim way of life. So you can see from this that I don't really mind if people call me an imam or a priest—I am both, but at different times. Does that sound complicated to you?"

Peter: "Well, it does really, but I think I understand what you mean. Can you tell me who looks after the running costs of the mosque?"

Imam: "Each mosque has its own elected committee. This committee usually employs a permanent imam or priest while also looking after the financial side of the mosque."

Peter had asked many questions and had thoroughly enjoyed his visit. As he went out of the prayer-room he noticed a coin-operated telephone and a fire extinguisher in the entrance hall. He thought that both of these were sensible items to include in a building which is so often used by large numbers of people. As the boys were about to leave, the imam asked Peter to call again one day the

73

following week when the children were in the mosque's school so that Idris and Fatima would be able to show him what they studied in the mosque's classes.

INTERNAL APPEARANCE OF NON-PURPOSE-BUILT MOSQUES IN BRITAIN

In such places of worship whether these be houses, modified shops, vicarages, churches and so on, Muslims try to create the atmosphere of purpose-built mosques whenever possible. Hence mosque features such as shoe-racks, washing and toilet facilities, prayer-hats, prayer-mats, agarbattis, prayer-boards, minbars and staffs, calligraphy and so forth may be seen in many such buildings. One important Islamic feature which is not easily created in non-purpose-built mosques is a mihrab facing the direction of the Qibla. Muslims often compromise on this by using a prominent part of the room, such as a window or doorway, as a mihrab. If this happens to be facing the Qibla, then so much the better. Only a window or doorway facing Mecca would be used.

9 Guidance for Children

When Peter went back to the mosque to see the children at their lessons he had to go upstairs. Here he saw not only the imam's living quarters (one room and a kitchen) but a number of class-rooms, each partitioned off with sliding doors.

In purpose-built mosques Muslims prefer to divide off their class-rooms with sliding doors, temporary partitions and curtains. These may be moved back on occasions to make space for a big room capable of accommodating a large number of worshippers. Such a room is needed for two reasons. First, when the prayer-room is unable to hold all the men who have come to the mosque. And second, when women come to pray.* The occasions when this large room is used are generally on special celebrations or when notable Muslims from other towns or countries are visiting the mosque. Extension speakers are used to enable the upstairs listeners to hear what is being said.

In non-purpose-built mosques, however, Muslims are often unable to achieve this extra large dual-purpose room, but where possible the buildings are adapted; for instance, walls are often knocked down to provide this facility.

Peter was surprised at the furniture used in the mosque's class-room. He had expected to see desks and other fittings such as he was used to at his school. Instead, he learned that Muslim children knelt at low benches for long periods at a time. Some of the benches he saw were smooth and well

*See Chapter 5 for more details concerning women in mosques.

finished, but others were roughly constructed. Whilst the teachers had benches similar to those used by the children, as instructors they were free to stand up and stretch their legs by walking around the class-rooms as lessons proceeded. The furniture found in the mosque the Husseins attend is similar to that found in many British mosques.

Fatima told Peter that Muslim children started to come to the mosque's classes from the age of five. She would stop coming to the classes when she was twelve—she would then be considered "grown-up". Peter was interested to hear that Fatima had never been allowed to go into the prayer-room— that was the prerogative of Muslim males.

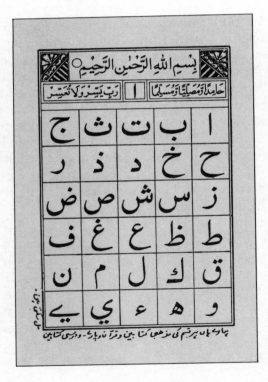

Arabic alphabet

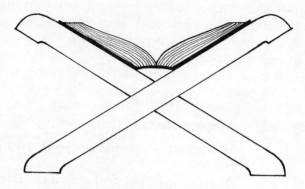

The Qur'an raised above the floor

Idris, however, still attends the mosque's classes. While many of his peers left the mosque's classes at the same time as the girls, Mr Hussein wants Idris to go until he reaches the age of fifteen. The class in which Idris is at present is smaller than those catering for children in the five to twelve age group. Mosque classes in Britain generally begin at 5 p.m. and last for some three hours per night (two and a half in winter) for five nights a week. A minority of British mosques require week-end attendance from their children, but Idris and Fatima do not have to attend at week-ends.

British mosques, in common with many mosques throughout the world, teach Islamic studies in their classes.* They do this by teaching Urdu (the national language of Pakistan which is much used in the Indian subcontinent) and Arabic (the language of the Qur'an), using appropriate language primers. The Qur'an and religious books about the life of Muhammad (written in Urdu) are also studied.

*Mosques in Islamic countries do not need classes for children—Islamic studies is taught on a compulsory basis in schools. In fact, if a pupil in Pakistan fails to pass Islamic studies he is considered to have failed his course of secondary education.

The imam and teachers at the mosque Idris attends have developed a syllabus for each of their mosque's classes. This syllabus is generally typical of the type of curriculum followed in mosque classes in Britain.

Syllabus

Age of child	Subjects studied
5 +	Introduction to the mosque and its routine.
6 +	Arabic alphabet and primer started.
7 +	Thirtieth part of the Qur'an read and memorised. This is the last part of the Qur'an which, owing to its short sections, is considered to be the easiest introduction for children. *
8 +	Beginnings of the Qur'an. Life of the Prophet read.
9 +	Qur'an parts 1–4 plus religious teaching.†
10 +	Qur'an parts 5–12 plus religious teaching.
11 +	Qur'an parts 13–20 plus religious teaching.
12 +	Qur'an parts 21–30 plus religious teaching.

*As a mark of respect and reverence for the Qur'an, Muslims generally make sure that it is raised from the floor when being read. During lessons, children place their Holy Book on their benches. Where this is not possible, or when an adult Muslim wishes to read from the Qur'an, a bookstand is often used. Ensuring that the Qur'an is raised from the floor is necessitated by the fact that Muslims often read in a sitting position.

†Mosques often differ in the texts used for religious teaching, but the overall content is similar in most mosques—it covers mosque routines such as prayer as well as books concerning Muhammad and Islamic customs.

Children attending the mosque are often guided with prayer times by the use of a prayer-card

Idris told Peter that only the thirtieth part of the Qur'an is learned off by heart in the mosque's classes, the rest being recited normally. It is only the few boys such as himself who progress to learn more of the Qur'an off by heart after the age of twelve. Idris, in common with many other Muslim children in Britain, has learned both the Arabic and Urdu languages. In Arabic the main emphasis has been on oral work for the purpose of reading the Qur'an. In Urdu, however, the emphasis is slightly different because Muslim children are not only required to read religious books written in Urdu but are also expected to speak the language fluently.

Peter was surprised when he realised how much Muslims study the Qur'an. He thought that Idris must know more about the Qur'an and his religion than he himself knew about Christianity. In fact, Peter was unable to quote much from the Bible except the Lord's Prayer, which he recites in school each day, and Psalm 23, which he sometimes sings at church.

A common feature in most British mosques is the examination of the children's ability in Islamic studies. Some mosques, like the one Idris attends, hold an annual examination, whereas others hold them more frequently, perhaps twice or three times a year. All Muslim children are required to pass these examinations in order to progress to the next class. In practice, however, few children fail. The end of the year for mosque classes in Britain is usually considered to be the end of Shahban. Hence children change classes after the Ramadan holiday.

Examinations in British mosques are usually given to the children individually. They often consist either of reciting prayers, performing rituals or reading in Arabic or Urdu. The examiner is usually an invited representative from another mosque. He may be an imam or any well-respected member of the Muslim community to which he belongs.

Few Muslim teachers at British mosques are qualified in Islamic studies. Those who are, generally hold the position of imams at a mosque. Most mosque teachers in Britain are volunteer Muslims who are considered by their particular Muslim communities to be sufficiently grounded in Islamic studies to be able to teach it.

It used to be difficult for British Muslims to gain a teaching qualification in Islamic studies once they had entered Britain. This situation has now changed because an Islamic College, opened in Lancashire in 1975, now trains Muslims to gain Islamic teaching qualifications.

Peter had found his visits to the mosque classes extremely interesting. Of all the practices which surprised him, none did so more than the fact that Muslim children always obey their teachers. Peter knew that his own teacher at school sometimes had to wait a long time for the class to be silent, but here at the mosque a teacher only had to speak and all the children were immediately quiet. Peter was told that the teachers at Idris's mosque used a cane in order to keep strict discipline. Muslim parents agree with the teachers that discipline is a necessary part of the Islamic religion, for it encourages respect towards teachers and parents as well as towards the supreme authority of Allah.

A.M.F.I.B.—F

10 Marriage

Marriages in the Muslim community are still arranged, although they only take place with the consent of both parties. Courting is absolutely forbidden.

Mr Hussein told Peter one day that all Muslims are expected to marry. The age at which they are encouraged to do so depends on the civil law operating in the country in which the Muslims concerned happen to be living.

Peter: "Where did you get married, Mr Hussein?"

Mr Hussein: "In Pakistan. Weddings there are quite simple. In the presence of four witnesses (two is the minimum allowed) Mrs Hussein and I recited certain passages from the Qur'an. Then we both repeated our consent to the marriage. We did this three times. After the ceremony the imam and guests prayed for us. Cups of tea and light refreshments were provided, the whole procedure lasting only a few minutes."

Peter: "Do British Muslims marry in this way?"

Mr Hussein: "No, at the mosque I now attend in Preston, the bride remains at home while the bridegroom goes to the mosque for the wedding ceremony. Although the bride does not attend the ceremony, she appoints an agent and usually two others to represent her. The agent and the two witnesses hear the girl acknowledge three times that she is willing to be married. They do this at the girl's home. They then go to the mosque, along with the bridegroom and members of the local community. The imam asks the bridegroom three times if he is willing to marry the girl in question, and then asks the bride's representative if the bride is willing to marry the bridegroom at this ceremony. If both sides give affirmative replies, the couple are married.

"Perhaps I ought to mention, Peter, that Muslims in Britain are obliged to marry in a civil wedding at a registrar's office in addition to the religious ceremony I have just mentioned. This is to make the wedding comply with the laws of the land."

Peter: "Do Muslims give wedding presents?"

Mr Hussein: "Yes, they often do, but on a much smaller scale than many English families. More important than these is the dowry the bridegroom has to give the bride. This is based on the bridegroom's means and the bride's position in society. The maintenance of the wife and her children is the duty of the husband, even though the woman may be wealthy."

Peter: "Is it true that Muslims can have more than one wife?"

Mr Hussein: "Yes, Muslims may have up to four wives. However, no Muslim can take on a second wife unless he is capable of doing so. A Muslim who contracts two marriages must treat both wives the same, materially and in every other way. He must also have the permission of his existing wife and that of his proposed new wife before he takes on a second marriage contract.

"Another point here is that Muslims obey the laws of the land in which they live. Therefore Muslims in Britain can only have one wife to comply with the law. Similar laws restricting Muslims to one wife are to be found in certain Islamic countries. So you will see from this that Muslims generally have only one wife."

Peter: "Is divorce permitted in Islam?"

Mr Hussein: "If marriages do not work out, divorce is allowed as a last resort. Muslims believe that divorce is hateful to Allah, but either party has the right to seek one. Three criteria must be met before divorce is allowed. First, both parties must try to solve the problem. Second, if unsuccessful, two relatives or close friends, one from each side, must be appointed to try to settle the differences. And finally, a four-month period must have elapsed before the marriage is terminated. After a divorce there is a waiting time during which the divorcees are not permitted to re-marry.''

Peter: "Did Muhammad marry?"

Mr Hussein: "Yes, he had many wives—some say he had as many as fourteen. Nine of his wives outlived him.''

Peter: "Can Muslims marry non-Muslims?"

Mr Hussein: "Yes, mixed marriages are permitted in Islam, but the regulations differ for males and females. A Muslim boy can marry a Jewish or Christian girl, although it is desirable that she should be converted to Islam first. Non-Jewish or non-Christian women, for example Hindus and Sikhs, must be converted to Islam prior to marriage. Muslims regard Jews and Christians as being nearer to their beliefs about Allah than are those who worship idols. However, a Muslim girl is not permitted to marry anyone but a Muslim boy.''

Peter had found this conversation with Mr Hussein very enlightening. He was beginning to feel now that he understood more about his friend Idris and the Hussein family.

11 Death

When a Muslim dies there are a number of rites to be observed. These are not to be found prescribed in the Qur'an but in law books. The latter sometimes disagree about ritual.

There are more differences in rites for Muslims living in Britain than elsewhere. This is for two reasons. First, mosques differ in the provision they make for the dead. For instance, a purpose-built mosque such as that which the Husseins attend is better able to supply facilities with regard to this matter than is a non-purpose-built mosque, which may just be a room in someone's terraced house. Second, local authorities vary in the provision they make for Muslim burials. For example, in 1975 only fifty-one local authorities in England and Wales provided Muslims with a separate burial plot in their cemeteries.

Ideally, Muslims prefer to have their own plot in the cemetery, a specific alignment of graves, one body to a grave, and the grave raised a little above the ground to prevent anyone walking on it.

In some places in Britain Muslims are able to observe most of the above criteria, the usual exception being that each grave has to contain more than one body. Too much land would be taken up otherwise.

Muslims like to prepare fellow Muslims' bodies prior to their going to a British undertaker.

The dead body is placed on a stretcher with the head in the direction of the Qibla. A major ritual washing (**ghusl**) follows. Soap and sweet-smelling substances such as

85

camphor are used during the ghusl, after which the body is wrapped in a shroud, placed in a coffin, and given to the undertaker. Whilst British law requires coffins to be used for burials, Muslims in Pakistan and India do not use them. Instead, they place the body in the ground, protected by planks of wood and then covered over with earth.

For the funeral a salat is performed in either the house of the dead Muslim or in the mosque. This is like an ordinary salat except that it includes prayers for the dead.

A general rule with regard to the time of burial is that it should take place as soon as possible after death. British Muslims generally aim for the day after death, but because of the difficulties over week-end funerals this is not always possible. In fact, some Muslims prefer their dead to be flown back to Pakistan or India to be buried, if it is felt that by so doing the burial will take place more quickly. This is especially the case when public holidays such as Christmas cause burial delays in Britain.

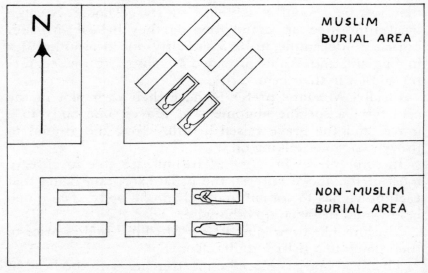

Cemetery showing the different burial positions for Muslims and non-Muslims

86

Muslims believe that the body should be buried with the face to the right and facing Mecca. A grave in Britain should therefore run north-east to south-west, with the head at the south-west end, facing right.

SUGGESTIONS FOR FURTHER STUDY

1   Try to arrange a visit to a mosque. Write to the secretary of the mosque committee to make arrangements. When you visit a mosque, take note of both the external architecture and the interior rooms, etc. You could then develop your own project booklet on a British mosque with the information you have gathered yourself. Other books and encyclopaedias would also help you.

2   Compare the preparations for prayer made by Muslims, Christians, Jews, Hindus and Sikhs.

3   To what extent do the different designs, size and furniture of mosques, churches, Hindu and Sikh temples give you an idea of the religion's idea of worship?

4   Compare a mosque school with your own, using the following headings: size of rooms, furniture, position of children, books used, variety in lessons, teachers.

5   Describe the similarities and differences between an English and a Muslim wedding.

6   The world's great religions have a wide variety of views on what happens to people after death. It is interesting to look for similarities and differences in these ideas. You might also prepare a questionnaire on what your class-mates think will happen to them after death.

12 Home Life

Mr Hussein came to Britain from Pakistan in order to find work and better his standard of living. He obtained employment in a textile factory. Many of the workers in Mr Hussein's factory are also from Asia. This is a common feature in Britain: a quarter of all Pakistani men are employed in the textile industry.

Mr Hussein works shifts, 2 p.m. to 10 p.m. one week, 10 p.m. to 6 a.m. the next, and 6 a.m. to 2 p.m. the following one. When he works on the night-shift nearly all the other employees are Pakistanis and Indians, but on the day-shift he also works alongside British workers.

The company which employs Mr Hussein has provided special facilities for those Asians who wish to fulfil their religious obligations, in particular that of praying at certain times of the day.

A special room has been made available which the Muslim workers have carpeted. In addition, a number of washing areas have been installed so that the workers can perform their ablutions before saying their daily prayers.

On the night-shift most of the conversation that takes place tends to be in Urdu, but on the day-shifts there is a great variety of language—English, Urdu, Gujarati and Punjabi being common. Some of the workers can speak as many as three different languages.

It is because of his contact with many English speakers in the textile mill that Mr Hussein has learned to speak English well, although he did know some before he came to Britain.

Mrs Hussein, on the other hand, knew very little English until a year ago. In this she is typical of many Muslim women who came to Britain to join their husbands but who have rarely had the opportunity to mix with and talk to English-speaking people. Only about two Muslim women in ten go out to work, in contrast to five out of ten among the Hindus and Sikhs, and seven out of ten among West Indian women.

The normal pattern is for Muslim women to remain at home and see to the running of the house. This is one reason why so many Muslim men work shifts, for with only one wage coming into the home they have to make sure they earn enough for all the needs of the family. In most factories shift work pays better than regular day work. Working permanent night-shift is the best-paid shift of all and consequently this is popular with many Muslims.

Although Mrs Hussein does not go out to work, she has decided that she needs to speak English. She asked her husband to check at the local Community Relations Office about help with the learning of English and he was able to discover that there are English classes available for Asian women, held in a schoolroom in the town. Some women can also have visits from a volunteer who helps them with English while they remain at home. Mrs Hussein has found this help of great value and she has made a number of good friends among the women who are learning with her.

Peter had noticed that when he first used to call for Idris everyone would be speaking in Urdu in the home. Idris explained to Peter at the time that this was because his mother did not understand English, and when the children spoke to each other in English she would tell them off, thinking that they must be planning some kind of mischief. Since beginning English lessons herself, Mrs Hussein no longer insists that the rest of the family should always speak in Urdu. Now she rather likes the chance to try out her English on her family, although whenever she wants something done quickly or is angry she starts to speak in Urdu again.

The Husseins live in a terraced house close to the centre of town. Mr Hussein is buying the house with the help of a mortgage from a building society. In this he is typical of many Asians who prefer to buy a house rather than rent one. Eight out of ten Asians live in their own homes, and only four out of a hundred live in council houses.

Many of the Husseins' neighbours are also Muslims. The Husseins, however, are a little different from many of them in that they have a smaller family than average. They have only two children, whereas many Muslim families have four or more. Some of these large families find it hard to manage and often live in houses that are smaller than they really need. A few families run into money problems, but when they do so a neighbour usually helps them out with a loan. Mr Hussein has helped one of his neighbours on two occasions, but he has never asked for any interest to be paid on the loan, for that is strictly against the principles of Islam. A private loan should be given as an act of good-will, and not in an attempt to make money.

The first time Peter had been invited into Idris's house he had expected to find it rather miserable because he had heard that Muslims do not like anything bright and cheerful in their homes. He found that just the opposite was the case. The walls were decorated with brightly coloured pictures and ornaments. There were paintings of Mecca and other holy places, wall plaques with Arabic writing on them, model peacocks with gaily coloured feathers and a wide variety of other decorations. All that was missing, just as in the mosque, were pictures or photographs of people.

The other surprise Peter received on his first visit was the way in which the children always did exactly as their parents told them. Peter was used to speaking his mind if he thought his parents were acting unreasonably, so he asked Idris why he never questioned what his parents said.

Idris explained that it was normal among Muslims that a child should obey his parents. He added that Mr Hussein

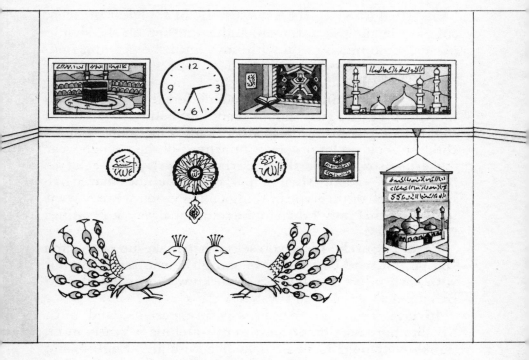

Wall decorations

would still obey his father if he were given an instruction. Idris admitted he was sometimes unhappy with things he was given to do, but nevertheless he would not argue with his parents.

Idris: "In many ways, Peter, my parents are much easier on Fatima and myself than are the parents of other Muslim children we know. Some parents don't allow their children to watch TV, because they don't approve of what is shown. My dad has had TV for as long as I can remember, and we can watch most things without too much trouble."

Peter: "My mum switches the telly off when there is a lot of swearing—she doesn't like my little sister to hear it. Is that the kind of thing Muslim parents object to?"

Idris: "It's partly that, but there's more to it. Muslims believe that when a girl reaches the age of twelve or thirteen, she is growing into a woman, and from then on she should not have too much to do with boys until she gets married. Once married she should keep herself covered up—except to her husband.

"Not all Muslims are equally strict on this, but they do tend to agree that girls should keep their bodies covered and should not go out on dates with boys. They don't like us children seeing a lot of television where all the women wear make-up, some wear short skirts and girls have a lot of boy-friends. Some Muslim parents are afraid that if we see too much of this type of thing on television we may want to live like that rather than in the traditional way our families would prefer."

Peter: "Surely, Idris, you see girls in make-up every time you go out, and you see boys and girls who are going out with each other at school. So you know life is like that in Britain even if you don't watch TV."

Idris: "Yes, and that is why my parents, and most Muslim parents, don't object to us watching TV. My mum thinks watching TV will help her with her English and Dad won't leave the telly when there is cricket on, particularly a test match between England and Pakistan.

"Even so, what you said about school is interesting, because many Muslim parents in various parts of Britain are not happy sending their daughters to secondary schools which have boys and girls in the same building.

"My own parents are not too bothered because they feel they have taught us to behave in the way they would expect, and they hope that by mixing with boys and girls we will fit into British society more easily. Other parents are not so sure they can trust their children and they would like to see special schools opened for girls aged between thirteen and sixteen.

Peter: "It's not too bad at our school, is it, Idris? Muslim girls wear slacks under their skirts and they do P.E. and go to the baths at different times from the boys."

Idris: "But not all schools are like ours, and anyway it is the mixing of boys and girls at playtime and lunch-time that worries many Muslim parents."

Peter: "Why is it only the girls who need to be treated in this way? There seems to be a definite difference between the way boys are treated and the way girls are expected to act."

Idris: "I wondered when you would ask that. It is the thing British people always say—that girls are always kept in the house while the men have all the freedom.

"The way women behave is based on what is written in the Qur'an:

'Men are in charge of women, because Allah has made one of them to excel the other, and because they spend of their property [for the support of women].' (Surah 4, verse 34)

"That is why my father goes out to work and my mother doesn't. My father earns the money to support the family, but Mother runs the home. She taught us all about our religion when we were little. She taught us how to speak Urdu, how to pray, and she still gives us jobs to do around the house. My dad never interferes with the way she runs the home. It is Allah who says our mothers should not go out unless fully covered, and Muslim women follow the instructions they read in the Qur'an:

'. . . tell the believing women to lower their gaze and be modest . . . and to draw their veils over their bosoms. . . .'" (Surah 24, verse 31)

It was not the question of the way children treat their parents nor the wishes of parents for their daughters that Peter found most fascinating. It was the way he had never been asked to wait outside the house when calling for Idris, and the way he was always invited to stay for a meal, or at least a cup of tea, that intrigued Peter most. Muslims regard it as a duty to offer hospitality to visitors and are always delighted when the offer is accepted. When Peter had become a regular visitor to Idris's home, Mr Hussein decided to tell him about an old custom which all Muslims observe on visiting.

The right side of the body is the side which performs all the actions which are pleasurable, whereas the left side of the body performs those which are unpleasant. Entering someone's home is a pleasure, so it is traditional to enter with the right foot. To leave a home is unpleasant so Muslims leave with the left foot first. Peter is not a Muslim, but now he always enters the Husseins' house with his right foot first to show that he regards it as a pleasure to visit them.

13 Dress

In explaining that women ought to be covered up, Idris had touched upon the subject of dress. There is considerable variety in the clothing worn by Muslims, and while some of the rules governing dress are distinctly Islamic, others tend to have their origins in more locally based customs.

When Peter visited the mosque, he gained a good idea of the type of clothes which are regarded as appropriate for the salat. The more orthodox among the congregation favoured a seamless white overshirt, white cotton trousers and a white cap. There is a tradition that the Prophet insisted that worshippers should not wear brightly coloured clothing, as this was liable to distract others from their prayers.

The majority of men do not wear all white, nor do they wear bright clothing. The normal pattern is for worshippers to pray in their everyday clothes, or alternatively in their pyjamas.

There are a number of restrictions as to what men may wear, and chief among these is a ban on the wearing of silk. Likewise, men should not wear anything made of gold, although objects made of silver, such as rings, are allowed.

Many men sport a beard, because the Prophet is reported to have worn one. Imams in particular are likely to have a beard. Among the general congregation, however, there are as many clean-shaven as there are bearded men.

The word "humility" best sums up the attitude expected

95

of a good Muslim. Muslims will often say that a man should not be proud, as pride is only for Allah.

There is a certain degree of regulation too in clothes worn by women. Some women come from parts of Pakistan where it is the custom to cover the whole of the face when leaving the house, and many continue this practice after settling in Britain.

However, most Muslim women prefer not to cover their faces completely and instead wear a scarf over their hair, just like many British women, and sometimes they keep a piece of material across the lower part of the face. The trend is very much towards wearing nothing over the face, with just a headscarf fastened under the chin. Yet it is rare to see a Muslim woman with her head completely uncovered.

What a woman chooses to wear will depend on a number of factors. First, it is dependent on where she lived before coming to Britain—women from towns cover up less than women who come from remote villages. Second, there is the influence of the neighbours. If all the Muslim women in the area cover their faces, then the newcomer will do likewise; whereas if the neighbours simply wear scarves, then the newcomer will probably do likewise. Muslim women, like men and women all around the world, are likely to dress in a similar style to their friends. In the same way, many young British people prefer one brand of jeans to another, or one kind of hairstyle. The third factor affecting dress is the length of time the woman spends in Britain and the contact she has with other cultures, and therefore with other forms of dress.

Mrs Hussein has noticed that these factors come into play when Muslims discuss whether certain items of clothing are permissible. She sometimes wears clothes that are bright red, and many of her friends do likewise. Mr Hussein regards this as perfectly all right, and he also approves of his wife wearing silk. But other husbands regard silk as wrong for women as well as men, and many consider red to be an inappropriate colour for a woman to wear.

When girls go to the mosque for lessons there is general agreement that their headscarves should be white, but even then some girls go in headscarves of various colours.

A few Muslim women wear **saris**, but Mr Hussein does not approve of his wife wearing one and so she never does. He feels the sari shows off a woman's figure too much and therefore it is not the correct form of dress for a woman, who must always be modest in her appearance.

The most favoured form of dress for girls and women is a **shalwar**. These are pants which are tight around the ankle, but baggier higher up. They are often worn with a **kameez**, which is an overdress, usually reaching to just above the knees.

The one aspect of dress which does cause arguments is what to wear on the wedding-day. Mr Hussein is not too troubled by the disputes which surround this topic. He regards it as a problem which has arisen because of the demands of young people and a higher standard of living.

Mr Hussein was married in the simple clothing that a worshipper is expected to wear in the mosque. Most of his generation dressed like this. However, many of the young Muslim men who get married in Britain prefer to buy a new suit, shoes, shirt and tie and to dress just as a British bridegroom would.

The Muslim bridegroom wears his new clothes when he goes to the registrar to perform the civil wedding. A week later, when he goes to the mosque for the religious ceremony, he sometimes runs into arguments with his older relatives.

Mr Hussein thinks that the matter should not lead to unhappiness at the time of the wedding and he is content to see a young man go to the mosque in smart new clothes. Nevertheless, he does believe that a dark suit is preferable to a bright one, and he would not agree to a bridegroom wearing a silk shirt or a silk tie—that would be going too far. Many older Muslims accept that a young man wants to look his best on his wedding-day and they acknowledge that

97

The shalwar and kameez

a better standard of living makes it possible for a bride-groom to afford a good suit. In a few families, however, this can cause a great deal of upset.

Peter remarked to Idris that he had always believed that Muslim women should not wear jewellery. This did not surprise Idris, because it is a common error among those who do not know many Muslim families. Mrs Hussein and Fatima both wear jewellery, although again it is a matter of personal choice—women don't have to if they do not wish. The most common type of decoration is the bracelet—some girls wear eight or nine on each wrist. Many women also wear earrings, and a large number use perfume (as do men in the mosque).

Some of the girls decorate their hands with **henna**, which is an orange dye. A few girls use it regularly, but Fatima only puts it on when it is an Id or when there is a wedding.

14 Food

"Forbidden unto you [for food] are carrion and blood and swine flesh, and that which hath been dedicated unto any other than Allah, and the strangled, and the dead through beating . . . whoseoever if forced by hunger, not by will, to sin: [for him] lo! Allah is Forgiving, Merciful." (Surah 5, verse 3)

There are a number of verses in the Qur'an which give details of the types of food banned for believers. The verse quoted here includes some of the prohibited food.

Mr Hussein, as a practising Muslim, is very careful to comply with all the demands made in the Qur'an and to ensure that the family do not break the religious laws.

Mr Hussein had to explain to Peter that the word **carrion** means any meat which comes from an animal that has not been killed in a special way. It is therefore forbidden for a Muslim to eat meat from an animal that has died from sickness or has been knocked down and killed.

The meat of most animals is permitted as long as the animal is killed according to the correct ritual. The cow (or sheep, etc.) must stand facing the Qibla (Mecca). The name of Allah is then pronounced. At the same time the animal's throat is cut and the blood allowed to drain away. This is done so that the blood is not eaten. British families normally eat meat which has had the blood cooked in it, but Muslims (and Jews) believe this to be unclean.

Parts of the body which consist of blood that does not

drain away (such as the liver) can be eaten by Muslims, whereas Jews are not allowed to eat the liver either.

Muslims in Britain can usually obtain their meat from a Muslim grocer or butcher. By so doing, they know that the animal has been slaughtered in the correct manner.

There are no prohibitions with regard to fish, which may therefore be bought from any fishmonger.

The one animal that people in the West eat a lot of, but which is forbidden to Muslims, is the pig. This means that a Muslim must not eat pork chops, pork steaks, pork pies, bacon or pork sausages, for the pig is regarded as unclean.

There are occasions when, even if meat has been drained of its blood, it should still not be eaten—for instance when the meat has been sacrificed to an idol. There is not much chance of this occurring in Britain, but in the past Muslim communities have had to take care not to buy meat that had reached a butcher's shop after being offered to a god as a sacrifice.

The one exception to the rule concerning the eating of forbidden meat is when a Muslim is in danger of starving. In that case, it is permitted to eat meat which would otherwise be prohibited—Allah will forgive.

This information prompted Peter to ask a question.

Peter: "On the occasions when you visit your friends, how can you be sure the food you are eating has been prepared in the correct way?"

Mr Hussein: "The short answer is that I cannot be sure. Even so I don't worry about it. I only eat in the homes of close friends who I know to be good Muslims, for of course they themselves would not eat unclean meat. This very problem arose centuries ago when hosts and their guests would argue about how clean the food was. It was decided then by Muslim leaders that, when a Muslim visits the home of another, he should not question the state of the meat but should just eat it. This is just what I do when I eat out."

In the same way that the Husseins eat only certain foods, they drink only permitted liquids.

In his early years as a prophet, Muhammad had a great deal of trouble with people who drank too much wine. At first, the Qur'anic laws told people to limit the amount they drank, especially before the salat:

> "O ye who believe! Draw not near unto prayer when ye are drunken." (Surah 4, verse 43)

This rule did not have the desired effect and so a stricter rule was introduced:

> "O ye who believe! Strong drink and games of chance . . . are only an infamy of Satan's handiwork. Leave it aside in order that ye may succeed." (Surah 5, verse 90)

Muslims in Britain follow this rule and do not have alcohol in the house.

It is interesting to note that the Husseins, like most of their Muslim friends, do not own a dog. The reason is connected with the laws concerning unclean food. The dog is generally regarded as an unclean beast. Should a dog lick a plate or any of the pans or dishes used for cooking and serving a meal, then the food is made impure and the pans and plates must be scrubbed clean.

Other traditions tell that an angel will never enter a house where there is a dog, and that the presence of one will ruin a salat.

Some Muslims do keep dogs, but even they would not keep a black one, for another tradition suggests that Satan sometimes disguises himself as a black dog.

Peter knew that Muslims are not supposed to drink alcohol, and he also imagined they were forbidden to smoke. Therefore he was amazed to see Mr Hussein smoking in his chair while watching his favourite TV programme, cricket.

It is true that some Muslims consider it is better not to smoke, but there is no rule about it. Mr Hussein agrees that it would be better if he didn't smoke, but he finds it very hard to give it up.

As the friendship between Peter and Idris grew, Idris began to have the occasional meal at Peter's. Peter was invited to Idris's house in return, but at first he wasn't too keen on going because he had heard that Asian food was odd to look at as well as being hot to eat.

Eventually Peter did agree to stay for a meal one evening, and he was pleasantly surprised with what he was given, although he did not like everything on the plate.

The family sat at the table and Peter heard them say the name of Allah in a short sentence before they started eating.

Peter was seated to the right of Mrs Hussein and she passed him a plate of **chapattis** so he could take one and pass on the remainder. Peter passed the plate back across the table, but Idris told him that it was customary for the plate to travel around the table going to the right each time. Mr Hussein told Peter that it didn't matter but that he thought he would like to know about such things just the same, because he was always asking questions.

When Peter picked up his cup with his left hand it was Fatima's turn to tell him not to use that hand for drinking. Mr Hussein explained why.

Mr Hussein: "The Prophet said, 'When one of you eats, let him eat with the right hand, and if he drinks he should drink with the right, for Satan eats and drinks with the left hand.'"

It was obvious to Peter yet again that a Muslim lives his life according to the laws and traditions of Islam, and these cover almost every aspect of life, including eating and table manners.

The Husseins used to eat with their fingers when they first arrived in Britain, but nowadays they eat far more Western dishes and so they sometimes use a knife and fork.

Fatima and her mother do most of the shopping. Mrs Hussein is best at buying Asian foods from Indian and Pakistani grocers, while Fatima is better at finding bargains in the supermarkets, especially when the weight is given in grams and not in pounds and ounces.

The Husseins eat far more potatoes than they used to, even more so since Idris started eating at friends' houses, where he developed quite a taste for chips. He also eats chips at school dinners, but Fatima has not had the chance to try school chips because she does not stay for dinners. Mr Hussein will not let her stay because she attends a primary school where there is no choice of food and meat is served four times a week. He says it is a waste of money for Fatima to stay. Idris is luckier. His school is a secondary school, where the pupils get a choice of food, so he usually manages a good meal without having to eat meat.

Mr Hussein cannot understand why his daughter has no choice when his son has a wide one, especially as both schools charge the same amount of money. Peter explained that it was because of the much larger size of the secondary school, but Mr Hussein was not convinced. He had recently visited a sick friend in hospital and found that the hospital provided a choice of food for Asian patients, so he hoped that before too long all the schools in which there were Asian children might also be able to offer a choice.

Peter enjoyed the meals he had with the Husseins and asked Mrs Hussein if she would write down a few of the recipes so that his mother could cook them for his family. Mrs Hussein was only too pleased to be asked and she provided Peter with a number of simple recipes.

Here are some which are easy to make:

CHAPATTIS
Ingredients:
1 lb (454 grams) wheat flour
2 tablespoonfuls of cooking oil
Directions: Mix the flour and oil in a bowl and add enough hot water to produce a dough. Press the dough into small balls and then roll them very flat. Grill them until brown. Add butter and serve.

Chapattis

POTATO BALLS
Ingredients:
1 onion
1 lb (454 grams) peeled potatoes
¼ lb (113 grams) grain flour
1 teaspoon lemon juice
1 teaspoon chilli powder
1 teaspoon salt
1 teaspoon mixed spices
1 teaspoon baking powder
Directions: Boil and mash the potatoes. Add salt, chilli powder, onion (chopped), lemon juice and the mixed spices. Roll the potato mixture into small balls. Prepare the batter, by using the grain flour and adding water, salt, chilli powder and baking powder. Add the water little by little—the batter must not be too watery. Dip the potato balls in the batter. Deep fry in cooking oil.

PEAS AND POTATO CURRY
Ingredients:
1 lb (454 grams) potatoes
½ lb (227 grams) fresh peas
pinch of mustard seeds
½ teaspoon chilli powder
½ lb (227 grams) tomatoes
cooking oil

105

Directions: Peel the potatoes and boil. Warm the mustard seeds in cooking oil (about 6 tablespoonfuls). Add the tomatoes, chilli powder and some salt to taste. Stir and heat gently. Add the peas and potatoes. Simmer for 15 minutes. Serve.

N.B. If fresh vegetables are expensive or scarce you can substitute frozen peas and tinned tomatoes. If you like your meals very hot, just add more chilli powder. Keep a glass of water handy, just in case!

15 Muslims in Britain

The Husseins are just one family among many who practise the religion of Islam in Britain. There are now well over half a million Muslims living in the United Kingdom. Many of them were born here and some are the children of parents who were born here—that is, second generation British Muslims.

It is no longer correct to regard the Muslim religion as a religion of immigrants. The Muslim community includes a large number of people who regard themselves as British but choose to follow the religion of their parents and grandparents, and indeed the British people pride themselves on the freedom available in this country for men and women to worship.

The large Muslim community has begun to add a new variety to the British way of life and the British high street. Most large towns have shops and companies which display strange names. There are banks, estate agents and solicitors who specialise in providing services for particular groups in our society. There are also grocers and greengrocers who provide foods and fresh fruit not previously available in Britain.

In the past it was possible for an English speaking person to travel to such diverse locations as Rome, Nairobi, Bombay and Singapore, and in each city to find himself a locally produced newspaper printed in English. Today, foreign language newspapers are published for Muslims in a mixture of Urdu and English or Gujarati and English, for many of the young people who want to read about the activities of

Muslim communities cannot read Urdu and so have to be provided with an English translation.

Aspects of British culture, particularly in areas such as education, government, language and law, have been assimilated into the cultures and institutions of nations as far apart as America and Japan, or Nigeria and Burma. This exchange of ideas is a two-way process and those people who spread British culture around the world returned with habits learned from abroad. Potatoes, tobacco and tea—three pillars of the British way of life—have all been introduced into this country from around the world since the age of exploration began.

The influx of Indian and Pakistani Muslims adds further variety to this "British" way of life, in the same way that Poles, Hungarians, Ukrainians, Czechoslovaks, Jews, Flemings, and even Normans, have in the past.

In most areas of Britain some aspect of the cultures of all these groups has been integrated into what we now regard as British culture. There are Saxon and Norman churches which we regard as a part of British history. The architecture of East Anglia is influenced by the styles common in the Low Countries. Orthodox (Greek and Russian) churches are thriving in Britain, adding to the variety within the Christian community of this country.

Similarly, the Muslims are making a mark on the architectural face of Britain. The most obvious example is the Regent's Park Mosque, one among many mosques being built, incorporating styles hitherto found chiefly in North Africa.

British society will undergo further changes in the future. Some factories may choose to operate a six-day working week with Fridays off, particularly during the month of Ramadan. In the same way, shops owned by Jewish business men choose to open from Sunday to Friday and close on Saturday.

Such changes will be accompanied by modifications within the Islamic communities here. English is already

108

beginning to replace Urdu, Punjabi and Gujarati in many homes—children may speak the language of their parents but they are increasingly unlikely to be able to read or write it fluently.

The availability of cheap and plentiful Western style clothing is also having its effects. Most men in this country, whether Christian, Jew, Hindu, Muslim, Sikh or atheist, wear a suit, shirt and tie. Children too dress alike, particularly boys.

The external differences are gradually disappearing and the hopes of people like the Husseins and Peter's family are centred upon the belief that other barriers can be removed. They hope that friendships which begin at school can last a lifetime and that people can live together in a multi-faith society without any one group ridiculing or condemning the beliefs and practices of others who follow different religions.

This book will, it is hoped, have given you an idea of what a Muslim is and what the religion of Islam teaches. What it cannot tell you is just how a Muslim feels about his God, for such feelings are very personal. To most Muslims Allah is a loving, caring father who provides for their every need. To some he is the judge on the last day. The best way to learn more about Islam is to talk to Muslim children about their religion and beliefs. No Muslim will refuse to tell you about his faith and his love of Allah. You are free to enter a mosque at any time in order to look around, although it would be reasonable to ask first rather than simply walk in. In reading this book you have scratched the surface of Islam. Now you should try to dig deeper.

SUGGESTIONS FOR FURTHER STUDY

1   Which aspect of the family life of a Muslim child would you most enjoy? Which would you find the most difficult to accept?

2   How far are British Muslims successful in preserving their own cultural identity as regards dress?

3   Prepare a day's diet for the Hussein family. Compare this with one you would prepare for an English family.

4   Collect cuttings from newspapers, magazines, etc., or visit your town or city centre and gather information which shows how immigrants are integrating into British society.

Glossary

agarbattis	incense sticks.
Allah	God.
azzan	recited by the muezzin when calling Muslims to prayer.
bedouin	dwellers in the desert (Arabian).
caliph	Muslim religious ruler; literally successor.
calligraphy	Arabic script: ornate handwriting.
carrion	meat coming from an animal which has not been killed in a special way.
chapatti	small flat cake of coarse unleavened bread.
ghusl	performed when preparing a Muslim for burial: major ritual ablution.
Hadith	a saying of the Prophet Muhammad.
Hajj	pilgrimage.
henna	orange dye used as a female cosmetic.
Hijra	Muhammad's move from Mecca to Medina; regarded as the starting-point of the Islamic era—hence A.H. (anno Hijra) is used as the reference-point in the Islamic dating system.
Id	festival.
imam	priest; a leader of congregational prayer.
Islam	religion followed by Muslims.
jamra	pile of stones representing Satan.
kameez	overdress reaching just above the knee; often worn with a shalwar.
khatib	person reading the Friday sermon.
mihrab	alcove marking the direction of prayer.

minaret	vertical tower of a mosque often capped with a miniature dome.
minbar	chair used during sermons, especially on Fridays.
mosque	Muslim place of worship.
muezzin	prayer-summoner: prayer-crier.
Muhammad	the prophet of Islam.
niya	statement of intent preceding a salat.
Qur'an	Holy Book of Islam.
Ramadan	month of the year in which Muslims fast.
Rashidun	the first four caliphs.
ruku	bowing position performed during a salat.
salam	greeting.
salat	prayer.
sari	length of cotton or silk worn as main garment by some Muslim women.
Sawm	Muslim fast.
Shahada	statement of faith.
shalwar	loose trousers worn by many Muslim women.
subhas	rosaries.
sujud	prostration position performed during a salat.
surah	chapter of the Qur'an.
tashahud	Muslim's profession of faith.
wuzu	washing before Muslim prayer: minor ritual ablution.
zakat	annual tax amounting to $2\frac{1}{2}$ per cent of a Muslim's savings which is distributed to the poor.